North Country Walks

By Keith Watson

Dedicated to Stan Cardwell, MBE

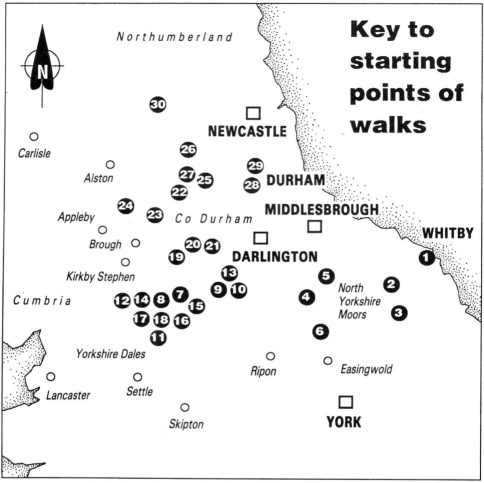

Key to starting points of walks

Northumberland

NEWCASTLE

Carlisle

Alston

Appleby

Brough

Kirkby Stephen

Cumbria

Yorkshire Dales

Lancaster

Settle

Skipton

Co Durham

DURHAM

MIDDLESBROUGH

WHITBY

DARLINGTON

North Yorkshire Moors

Ripon

Easingwold

YORK

Publisher's note

While every care has been taken in the compilation of this book, the publisher cannot accept responsibility for any inaccuracies or omissions. The countryside changes all the time — paths are sometimes diverted, hedges and fences can be removed, stiles disappear.

The maps in this book are based upon the Ordnance Survey Outdoor Leisure and Pathfinder maps with permission of the Controller of Her Majesty's Stationery Office. ©Crown Copyright.

Country Code

- Avoid damaging fences, hedges, walls.
- Fasten all gates.
- Guard against all risk of fire.
- Safeguard water supplies.
- Go carefully on country roads.
- Keep dogs under proper control.
- Keep to the paths across farmland.
- Leave no litter, take it home.
- Protect wildlife, plants and trees.
- Respect the life of the countryside.

Published by The Northern Echo, Priestgate, Darlington, Co Durham DL1 1NF
©The Northern Echo
ISBN 0 9515288 0 7 North Country Walks. (pbk)

Contents

Colour photographs: Cover views by David Frater
(front, Harforth; rear, West Layton)
All others by Tony Bartholomew.

Foreword

A rewarding by-product of country walking is the like-minded friends it brings us. Among these I value none more highly than Keith Watson. He enjoys hills and dales alike (neither could exist without the other) and, sporadically, flirts discreetly with the challenge of mountains. His expertise was invaluable during research for one of my books and it is a privilege to recommend his own — the consequence of years of booted exploration, an inquiring mind and a willingness to share his acquired knowledge. It was Keith who introduced me to Teesdale and adjacent splendours. These are not as widely appreciated as they should be. Britain's country walkers will be grateful to the author and The Northern Echo for this compendium which encapsulates Keith's gentle wisdom and unfussy affection for the nation's most popular recreation.

Reliable, detailed guidance to Keith's patch of countryside has never before been so neatly condensed into one volume. Generations yet unborn will benefit (as a host of us, notably Echo readers, already do) from his responsible advice. The author has done the groundwork. All his readers have to do is savour the fruits of it.

Hardened ramblers sometimes wander off the beaten tracks, the official public ways and improvise their own routes. But this practice can lead the inexperienced into trouble from which they may have to be extricated by others. That does not happen in Keith Watson's company. He is mindful too that the hills and dales are sources of income for farmers and landowners whose priorities must be respected. Moreoever, we all need a well-informed guide when walking in areas alien to our experience. Such a guide can even enhance our pleasure on walks we thought we knew well.

This book — up-to-date because the author never stops walking — meets all those needs. Keith will be with you every step of the way because he has been there himself carefully recording the necessary detail. He has done for the North-East and North Yorkshire the kind of job that Wainwright began to do for the Lake District in the 1950s. They have much in common, not least their reflective natures and the meticulous craftsmanship of their text and illustrations. The Northern Echo's sphere now has its own Wainwright. His name is Watson and you will find him the best of companions.

Rex Bellamy

(Rex Bellamy, a Yorkshireman, was brought up on the edge of the Peak District, where he roamed the moors, climbed the edges and did voluntary work for the National Trust. Since 1956 he has worked for The Times as an award-winning sports and feature writer. His six books include The Peak District Companion and Walking The Tops.)

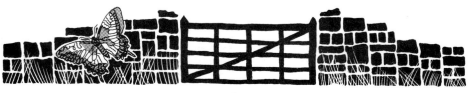

Introduction

This book is the result of requests from many readers of The Northern Echo who have expressed their appreciation of my popular weekly walks that have appeared in its columns. Encouraged by the tokens of interest, The Northern Echo has decided to publish in book form a selection of the walks from the series of 1988-89.

North Country Walks is indeed a fitting title with the walks dispersed throughout the North-East of England embracing Tynedale to Teesdale, including the Durham Dales coupled with the Yorkshire Dales and North York Moors.

For more than 30 years I have explored the undiscovered North Country. The only way to know this land, as every Northerner should, is to discover it on foot. Northerners are truly fortunate in having some of the finest dales on their doorstep.

The selection of walks, 30 in all, follow recognised public rights of way. Distances vary from three to 13 miles and some walks are quite short strolls and others longer, but all of them are easy to follow and suitable for most people of average fitness with moderate walking powers. All the walks are circular with convenient parking points and public transport details are listed wherever possible with every walk. The illustrated maps enhance the text and show the route, but you will need the required Ordnance Survey Maps which are listed with each walk.

Efforts have been made to indicate the best viewpoints and to enliven the walk with historic attractions. If the result is to give those who follow in my footsteps a share of the enjoyment which I have derived from these walks, the book will have served its purpose. The walks are offered, not as an exhaustive list, but as an introduction and I urge you to discover the North Country for yourself.

Finally, an earnest request to the new rambler and all walkers, remember the safety code and observe the Country Code.

Acknowledgements

First, my sincere thanks to the many readers of The Northern Echo who suggested that a collection of my walks should be combined into book form. Without their requests, this book might not have been possible.

Next, a special thank you to Allan Prosser, editor, and David Kelly, managing editor, of The Northern Echo for their help, support and co-operation in producing this volume. My congratulations to Mike Brough, graphic artist of the newspaper, for the final presentation of the excellent maps, and to Rex Bellamy for his encouragement. As a non-motorist, the use of cars made it easier to record the walks and I would like to thank Bert and David Adams of Billingham, Thomas Knox of Great Ayton, and David Thompson of Saltburn for helping me out with transport and being constant companions on the many miles recorded in this book.

Finally, I thank my wife Jean for helping me check the manuscript and tolerating my Saturday absences.

Keith Watson

(Keith Watson was born in Ferryhill, County Durham, in 1940 and now lives in Norton, Cleveland. He has been keenly interested in walking since the age of 18 and for the past 30 years has extensively walked throughout northern England. Author of two books — Walking in Teesdale and County Durham Walks for Motorists — he has written the popular walks column for The Northern Echo since 1980 and more recently in 1989 has contributed walk features covering the North York Moors for the monthly magazine Country Walking. A local government officer, he is married with two sons and a daughter.)

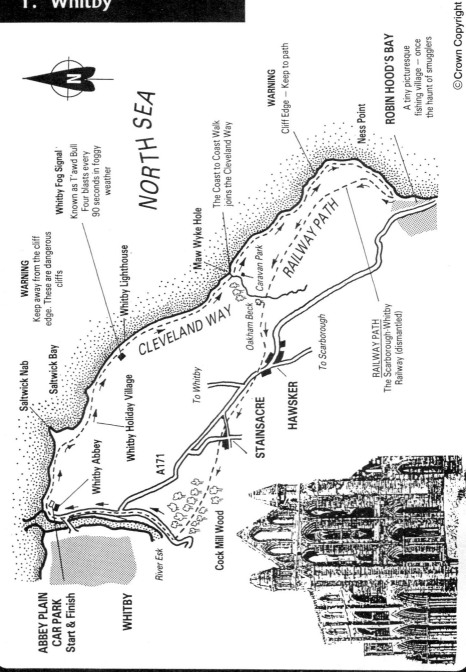

N

NORTH SEA

WARNING
Keep away from the cliff edge. These are dangerous cliffs

Whitby Fog Signal
Known as T'awd Bull
Four blasts every 90 seconds in foggy weather

WARNING
Cliff Edge — Keep to path

ROBIN HOOD'S BAY
A tiny picturesque fishing village — once the haunt of smugglers

Ness Point

The Coast to Coast Walk joins the Cleveland Way

Maw Wyke Hole

Whitby Lighthouse

CLEVELAND WAY

RAILWAY PATH

Caravan Park

Oakham Beck

Saltwick Nab

Saltwick Bay

Whitby Holiday Village

To Whitby

STAINSACRE

HAWSKER

To Scarborough

RAILWAY PATH
The Scarborough-Whitby Railway (dismantled)

Whitby Abbey

A171

Cock Mill Wood

River Esk

WHITBY

ABBEY PLAIN CAR PARK
Start & Finish

1. Whitby

Route: *Whitby — Saltwick Bay — Ness Point — Robin Hood's Bay — Railway Path — Whitby.*
Distance: *About 12 miles (19.5km). Allow 6/7 hours. Moderate. Easy to follow.*
O.S. Maps: *Landranger Sheet 94; Outdoor Leisure 27.*
Parking: *Abbey Plain Car Park, Whitby. Pay and Display.*
Public Transport: *buses — United Services Middlesbrough — Whitby; trains — Darlington/Middlesbrough/Whitby.*
Refreshments: *Plenty in Whitby and Robin Hood's Bay; Windmill Inn, Stainsacre.*
Warning: *Dangerous cliffs. Keep away from the cliff edge. Part of the cliff path is unfenced. Not advisable in wet and windy weather.*

THIS coastal circuit uses the Cleveland Way from Whitby to Robin Hood's Bay for a cliff top walk and highlights the spectacular scenery of Yorkshire's Heritage Coast. The return is along the disused Scarborough to Whitby railway known as the Trailway or Railway Path.

This walk starts opposite the impressive Whitby Abbey, founded in AD 657 by St Hilda, which is well worth a visit. From Abbey Plain car park, turn left along Abbey Lane and at Abbey Farm turn left through an unsignposted farm gate, pass the farm and follow the Cleveland Way to the coast path.

Head south along the well-used cliff path for about a mile to Saltwick Bay. It is easy to follow, fenced on either side and laid with duckboard.

When you see Saltwick Nab, the coal black nab jutting out into the sea, look for the shipwreck below. It was here in 1914 that the hospital ship Rohilla ran aground with 229 people on board — 85 were saved by lifeboat with 60 washed ashore.

Above Saltwick Bay, a Cleveland Way sign directs you through Whitby Holiday Village, a popular caravan and camp site. Beyond the site, keep along the signposted stiled coastal path with backward views to Whitby Abbey.

About a mile south of Saltwick Bay, pass in front of the whitewashed Whitby Fog Signal, nicknamed 'Whitby Bull' or 'T'awd Bull', which gives four blasts every 90 seconds in foggy weather. Avoid it in bad weather — it is deafening!

From the Fog Signal, bear half-right up the field to reach the entrance of Whitby Lighthouse (Private — no public right of way) where, by the gate, a sign marked "To Robin Hood's Bay" points left, up some steps and past the land side to the lighthouse. Follow the path up the hillside, and at the top admire the inland views to the moors.

Rejoin the well-used coastal path. Although easy to follow, it sticks closely to the edge of the cliffs, which are 200 to 300 foot high so be careful, especially in wet and windy weather. Sometimes there is a seaward fence and sometimes no protecting fence at all.

Below Northcliffe Caravan Park at Maw Wyke Hole, cross Oakham Beck, where Wainwright's Coast to Coast Walk joins the Cleveland Way, 187 miles from St Bees on the Cumbrian Coast.

Continue for the next three miles round Ness Point and Robin Hood's Bay comes into sight with spectacular views southwards to Ravenscar, perched 600 feet above sea level. Enter Robin Hood's Bay along Mount Pleasant North, which is also the exit for the return railway walk to Whitby. Turn left, steeply down the main street and explore the picturesque fishing village of Robin Hood's Bay with clustered cottages and seashore slipway. Once the haunt of smugglers, today it is a mecca for artists, fossil finders and tourists.

For the return, walk along Mount Pleasant North, where a signpost marked "Railway Path" directs you left up a rough road by some garages and turn right through a way-marked kissing gate with a notice "No motor cycles on this path" to join the Railway Path for Whitby. Follow the disused Whitby to Scarborough railway line for five and a half miles northwards with superb sea views. On the way, pass the villages of Hawsker and Stainsacre and proceed through Cock Mill Wood with magnificent views over the Esk Valley.

At the end of the walkway, go down the steps, turn left under the railway bridge and follow Larpool Lane to Whitby. Cross the A171 and along Church Street to climb the 199 steps to Abbey Plain car park.

2. Goathland

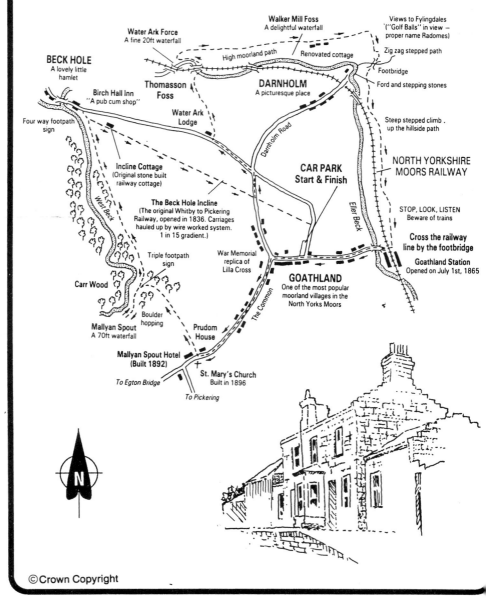

Walker Mill Foss
A delightful waterfall

Views to Fylingdales
("Golf Balls" in view —
proper name Radomes)

Water Ark Force
A fine 20ft waterfall

Zig zag stepped path

BECK HOLE
A lovely little
hamlet

High moorland path

Renovated cottage

Footbridge

Thomasson Foss

DARNHOLM
A picturesque place

Ford and stepping stones

Birch Hall Inn
"A pub cum shop"

Water Ark Lodge

Steep stepped climb .
up the hillside path

Four way footpath
sign

Darnholm Road

CAR PARK
Start & Finish

**NORTH YORKSHIRE
MOORS RAILWAY**

Incline Cottage
(Original stone built
railway cottage)

West Beck

Eller Beck

STOP, LOOK, LISTEN
Beware of trains

The Beck Hole Incline
(The original Whitby to Pickering
Railway, opened in 1836. Carriages
hauled up by wire worked system.
1 in 15 gradient.)

**Cross the railway
line by the footbridge**

Triple footpath
sign

War Memorial
replica of
Lilla Cross

Goathland Station
Opened on July 1st, 1865

Carr Wood

The Common

GOATHLAND
One of the most popular
moorland villages in the
North Yorks Moors

Boulder
hopping

Mallyan Spout
A 70ft waterfall

**Prudom
House**

Mallyan Spout Hotel
(Built 1892)

To Egton Bridge

St. Mary's Church
Built in 1896

To Pickering

N

8

2. Goathland

Route: *Goathland — Mallyan Spout — Beck Hole — Water Ark — Darnholm — Goathland.*
Distance: *3/6 miles. Fairly easy. Allow 1½ to 3 hours. Field and moorland paths with some stiff climbs.*
O.S. Maps: *Landranger Sheet 94; Outdoor Leisure Sheet 27*
Leaflets: *National Park Waymark Walk leaflets Numbers 14 and 15 obtainable from the shops in Goathland, 30p each.*
Parking: *Goathland Village car park — Beck Hole Road (GR 833013). Free car park.*
Public Transport: *United Services — Whitby to Goathland; Esk Valley Railway — Darlington/Middlesbrough/Whitby; North Yorkshire Moors Railway — Grosmont to Goathland.*

Goathland, one of the most attractive moorland villages in the heart of the North Yorks Moors, is a walker's paradise.

This short, easy walk around Goathland is a firm favourite with almost everyone. It includes a bit of everything — fields, woodland, moorland and waterfalls plus the Beck Hole Incline and spectacular views of the North Yorkshire Moors Railway.

From Goathland car park turn right and right again, along The Green, using the paved trod through the delightful village. Pass by the War Memorial (replica of Lilla Cross) and turn left along The Common for 880 yards to the extreme west end of the village.

Almost opposite St Mary's Church turn right and cross the stile. It is signposted "Footpath to Mallyan Spout" and follow the enclosed path along the grounds of the Mallyan Spout Hotel. Go down the railed path for a steep stepped descent into the wooded valley below. There are seats provided if you want a rest.

At the triple footpath signpost marked "Mallyan Spout/Goathland/Beck Hole" turn left upstream along the wooded West Beck with a small diversion to see the spectacular Mallyan Spout, a 70-foot waterfall — Goathland's highest waterfall. This 100-yard stretch of beckside path is strewn with large boulders, so expect some scrambling.

Return to the triple footpath sign and follow the Beck Hole route downsteam. Exit over a stile and out of the wood into the open pastures. The path is easy to follow, as it ascends four stiled fields with short stiff climbs and hugs the boundary fence of Carr Wood on your left.

Once you have gone down the zigzag stepped path, walk along the last field and out through a gate to reach the Beck Hole Incline. If you want, visit the lovely little hamlet of Beck Hole, branch left along the old railway line, then right along a gated bridleway to reach the six-house hamlet, whose pub-cum-shop Birch Hall Inn welcomes walkers.

Return to the Beck Hole Incline, pass Incline Cottage and walk up the old railway line (1:15 gradient), part of the original Whitby to Pickering railway engineered by George Stephenson and opened in 1836. Follow this uphill track for 440 yards to the Beck Hole road. Here you can shorten the walk and cross the road through the signposted gate and follow the rail trail back to Goathland.

For the longer walk, turn left along the road and at the crossroads continue along the Beck Hole road until you see a public footpath signpost on your right, just before the Water Ark Lodge. Turn right, cross the stile and along the enclosed path, cross another stile into the fields.

Go down the field edge fairly steeply and at the bottom cross a stile and descend the steps into the lovely valley of Eller Beck. Cross the footbridge over the beck which is actually situated underneath the railway bridge that conveys the North Yorkshire Moors Railway.

Here you will see Water Ark Pool, a deep and dangerous spot with a memorial reminder of Sidney Porritt, a 16-year-old youth who drowned in the beck on June 9, 1908.

Turn left alongside the railed fence and ascend the slanting moorland hillside path, with a glimpse of Water Ark Foss, a 20-foot waterfall. As you climb, you might be lucky to see the steam trains on the spectacular railway below.

From the hillside seat, bear right along the bracken path for a high level walk above Water Ark Scar, giving superb scenic views to Darnholm, Goathland and Fylingdales Radomes (golf balls), all visible. Look out for another waterfall called Water Mill Foss.

Follow the gated track, pass behind a renovated cottage and onwards through a gate, leave the track, bear right down through another gate and descend the steep bracken-covered hillside via some steep steps to cross a footbridge over the stream. Turn right along the road to the Eller Beck with its stepping stones and ford on the outskirts of Darnholm. Do not cross the beck, but turn left along a well-worn path for a stiff climb up the stepped hillside with the wall on your right.

The path levels out and splits right downhill and leads you to Goathland station. Cross the line by the footbridge and follow the road back to Goathland car park.

9

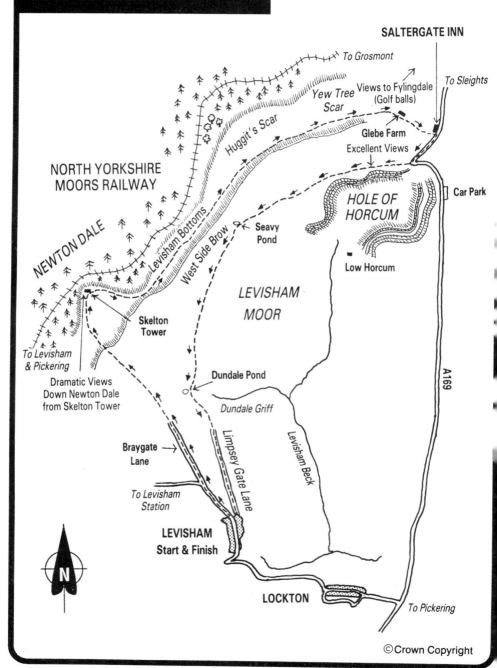

SALTERGATE INN

To Grosmont

Yew Tree Scar

Views to Fylingdale (Golf balls)

To Sleights

Huggit's Scar

Glebe Farm

Excellent Views

NORTH YORKSHIRE MOORS RAILWAY

HOLE OF HORCUM

Car Park

NEWTON DALE

Levisham Bottoms

West Side Brow

Seavy Pond

Low Horcum

LEVISHAM MOOR

Skelton Tower

To Levisham & Pickering

Dramatic Views Down Newton Dale from Skelton Tower

Dundale Pond

Dundale Griff

Braygate Lane

Limpsey Gate Lane

Levisham Beck

A169

To Levisham Station

LEVISHAM
Start & Finish

LOCKTON

To Pickering

N

© Crown Copyright

10

3. Levisham

Route: Levisham — Skelton Tower — Saltergate Inn — Seavy Pond — Dundale Pond — Levisham.
Distance: 7½ miles. Fairly easy. Allow 3/4 hours.
O.S. Maps: Landranger Sheet 94; Outdoor Leisure 27.
Parking: No car park in Levisham. Limited parking. Do not obstruct access for vehicles.
Refreshments: The Horseshoe Inn and The Old School House Tea Garden, Levisham. The Saltergate Inn.

This moorland walk combines history with legend and spectacular scenery with superb views. It is a little loop from Levisham over Levisham Moor to the old Saltergate Inn and back above the famous Hole of Horcum.

Leave Levisham at the top of the single street village and pass the Horseshoe Inn on your right. Walk up the metalled lane, do not turn left for Levisham Station, but continue straight on, northwards up the walled unsurfaced Braygate Lane with fine views of the heather-clad moor.

After 880 yards, cross a signposted stile by a gate marked "No unauthorised vehicles — keep dogs on lead", to reach Levisham Moor, part of the 2,100 acre estate purchased by the National Park Authority in 1976.

Here you will see a wayside information plate — "Levisham Estate — This land is owned by the National Park Committee and you are welcome to walk here. Please note that vehicles, metal detectors, guns, fires and tents are not allowed on the moor. We would be grateful if you would close gates after you and keep dogs on lead. — National Park Committee, North Yorks Moors."

Follow the track with the stone wall on your left and when the wall ends, stride out, straight on over the open moor to decend the moorland edge called West Side Brow and across the flat level Levisham Bottoms to Skelton Tower, a notable landmark overlooking the delightful secluded Newton Dale.

This ruined tower was originally a shooting lodge built by the Rev. Robert Skelton, Rector of Levisham in the early nineteenth century.

Local legend is divided as to whether he used this place for writing his sermons or as a place for a quiet drink. The tower was repaired and made safe in 1979 by the National Park Authority.

From this lofty spot, admire the excellent views and you might be lucky to see the steam trains on the North Yorkshire Moors Railway snake through Newton Dale.

Below West Side Brow and above Newton Dale, proceed northwards for 1½ miles on a broad moorland track with a gradual gradient, giving views on the horizon of Fylingdales 'golf balls.'

Keep on the main track, do not turn right below the ridge, but continue on and cross a stile by a green metal gate to leave the moor. Negotiate some stepping stones, bear half right along a rough pasture, cross a couple of stiles, pass Glebe Farm and climb up the stony track with an interesting slate notice "No bull in this field" to reach the busy A169 road.

Turn left to the Saltergate Inn, (formerly The Wagon and Horses which had its own tollbar in the eighteenth century) — an ideal halfway house for refreshments. This former smugglers' haven was situated on the old 'salt' road or fish road, from Robin Hood's Bay to Saltergate, where smugglers used to bring their fish to be 'salted' in the days of high salt tax. Hence the name.

From the pub, walk southwards by the grass verge, up the hairpin bend (known as The Devil's Elbow) on the busy A169 and near the top turn right and cross a signposted stile by a gate marked "No Model Flying Or Hang Gliding Except Under Licence — Please Keep Dogs On Lead" and re-enter Levisham Moor. Here admire the two way views to Flyingdales Ballistic Missile Early Warning Station and into the famous Hole of Horcum, nick-named the Devil's Punchbowl.

Local legend says that this large natural hollow was made by the legendary Giant Wade at the same time as Blakey Topping — the latter being the spadeful of earth whose robbery caused the Hole to come into being.

Another legend says that the creation of the Hole was the result of the Devil making the chasm into his Punch Bowl. Whichever you believe, it's still one of England's most spectacular viewpoints.

Follow the main moorland track south through an area associated with earthworks and an ancient boundary dyke. After a mile, pass Seavy Pond and continue south for another 1½ miles to reach Dundale Pond, where an information plate states: "This small valley was given to the Monks of Malton Priory in about 1230, as a pasture for their sheep, cattle and horses. Dundale Pond was probably made at this time as a place for stock to drink."

Continue up the track and at a signposted stile, leave the moor and walk down Limpsey Gate Lane for about a mile, back to Levisham village to end this splendid walk.

Solomon's Temple
Grass covered ruin remains of
Solomon Temple, once an ornate
farm built by Solomon Metcalfe

Chequers at Slape Stones

An old drovers' inn, now a working farm. See the restored sign:

Be not in haste,
Step in and taste,
Ale tomorrow —
For nothing'
Call in for refreshments

To Hawnby

Ruined farm

Join the Cleveland Way

THE HAMBLETON DROVE ROAD
An ancient drovers' highway

Unsuitable for motors

Slape Stones Beck

SHEEPWASH
A popular picnic spot
Start of the Lyke Wake Walk
and The Shepherd's Round

Crabdale Beck

To Swainby

Leave the Cleveland Way
and Coast to Coast Walk

Scarth Nick

Ford & footbridge

Steep Steps

Superb views

Scarth Wood Moor
(National Trust)

Cod Beck
Reservoir

White House
Farm

Green Lane

OAKDALE
A secluded valley with
twin reservoirs — the lower
one built in 1891 — the upper
reservoir built in 1910

Cod Beck

Quarry Lane

Beacon Hill
982 feet
Trig point top

Arncliffe Wood

CLEVELAND WAY

NOTICE
Take care
do not start
fires.

**British Telecom
Microwave
Radio Station**
A conglomeration of
aerial dishes and
metal gantries

Coast to Coast Walk joins
the Cleveland Way

South Wood

LADY'S CHAPEL
Built in 1515, restored
in 1960

Chapel Wood
Farm

Rueberry Lane

To A19

OSMOTHERLEY
Gateway to the
North York Moors
(START & FINISH)

To Thimbleby

Viewpoint Indicator
A tribute to Walter Evans, a
founder member, erected by the
Osmotherley Civic Society in 1980,
by kind permission of C. Bell Esq.

Extensive views over the
Vale of Mowbray to the
Pennines

4. Osmotherley

Route: *Osmotherley—Beacon Hill—Sheepwash—Chequers—Oakdale—Osmotherley.*
Distance: *About 7 miles (11 km). Easy/moderate. Allow 3½/4 hours. Some steep climbs.*
O.S. Maps: *Landranger Sheets 99 and 100; Pathfinder Sheets 621 (SE48/49) and NZ40/50.*
Parking: *No village car park. Limited roadside parking. Do not inconvenience residents.*
Public Transport: *United Services 290, Middlesbrough — Northallerton.*
Refreshments: *The Three Tuns Inn; Queen Catherine Inn; Golden Lion and The Coffee Pot in Osmotherley. Chequers Farm at Slape Stones.*

Here is a superb seven-miler and every mile a good one. This scenic walk uses the Cleveland Way which teams up with the Coast to Coast Walk for a climb over Beacon Hill, the highest point on the walk, with extensive panorama to the distant Pennines. Moorland tracks take you down to Scarth Nick for a road walk to the popular picnic spot of Sheepwash. Here you follow in the steps of the drovers along the Hambleton Drove Road with an invitation to drop in for tea at Chequers, the old Drovers Inn and now a working farm. The return route rejoins the Cleveland Way down in the secluded valley of Oakdale, for an all field path walk to complete a round trip back to Osmotherley.

From Osmotherley, walk up North End in the direction of Swainby and turn left into Rueberry Lane, signposted Cleveland Way and follow this unfenced and unsurfaced lane round Rueberry Hill. Where the lane divides at the Viewpoint Indicator, erected by Osmotherley Civic Society, there are extensive views over the Vale of Mowbray to the Pennine Dales.

For a short detour, take the upper track to the lovely Lady's Chapel, built in 1515 and restored in 1960, which is well worth a visit.

For the main route, walk along the lower track past Chapel Wood Farm which is on your left. Go through the waymarked, signposted kissing gate and follow the farm track through the gated fields into South Wood, where the Coast to Coast Walk comes up from Ingleby Arncliffe and encounters the Cleveland Way. Turn right at the Cleveland Way signpost for a stiff, steep climb up the forest drive which can be muddy even in summer.

At the top, walk along the wooded escarpment edge and pass the British Telecom Microwave Radio Station with its conglomeration of aerial dishes and metal gantries. When you see the white trig point — it is over the wall on your right — you have reached the summit of Beacon Hill (982ft), highest point on the walk.

Continue along by the wall, go through a gate, cross a corner stile and bear half right over Scarth Wood Moor (National Trust owned) with fine views over the Cleveland Hills to the Cleveland Plain, with Cod Beck Reservoir and Sheepwash seen below, and Black Hambleton southwards. Go down some steep steps to come out onto the road at Scarth Nick and turn right along this to Sheepwash, a popular spot where you can often buy an ice cream on summer weekends. It is the starting point for the Lyke Wake Walk and Shepherds Round.

From Sheepwash, ford or cross the footbridge over Crabdale Beck and then follow the broad track uphill. The route now follows High Lane, better known as the Hambleton Drove Road which runs south from Scarth Nick for 15 miles to Sutton Bank. Stride out and follow in the steps of the drovers along the ancient cattle highway for 1½ miles southwards to the Hawnby Road. Turn left along the road and in yards, on your left, note the grass covered remains of Solomon's Temple, once an ornate farm built by Solomon Metcalfe in 1812.

Continue down the road to Chequers and call in at the farm shop for tea and scones. This working farm, a former drovers inn was once famed for good ale, as proclaimed on the restored inn sign:

"Be not in haste, Step in and taste
Ale tomorrow for nothing"

Just beyond the farm, cross Slape Stones Beck and turn right at the public footpath sign and follow the track with the wall on your left. When the wall bends left, walk forward over the rough pasture and head downhill through a gate marked "Please Shut This Gate" on a green track into the hidden valley of Oakdale, with its twin reservoirs. Go through a gate, pass the derelict Oakdale House on your left and bear right down to the broad track below. You have now rejoined the Cleveland Way.

Turn right, cross a stile by a gate, pass the lower reservoir built in 1891 and follow the broad track uphill out of the wooded valley and along the fields to reach the Hawnby Road. Fifty yards down the road, turn right up Green Lane and beyond the entrance to White House, turn left over a stile signposted "Cleveland Way". Follow the farm road, pass White House on your left and aim for the telegraph pole marked with a large white arrow and the sign "Footpath" painted in bold white letters. Cross the stile, go down the hillside and cross the footbridge over the lovely wooded Cod Beck, known locally as Happy Valley.

Climb steeply out of the valley by the railed steps and at the top, proceed over a couple of stiled fields and along an enclosed path into Back Lane. Turn right, go by Bramblewick and St Anne's Cottage, via the cobbled path to pass Osmotherley Methodist Chapel dated 1754 and exit through Chapel Passage back into Osmotherley.

13

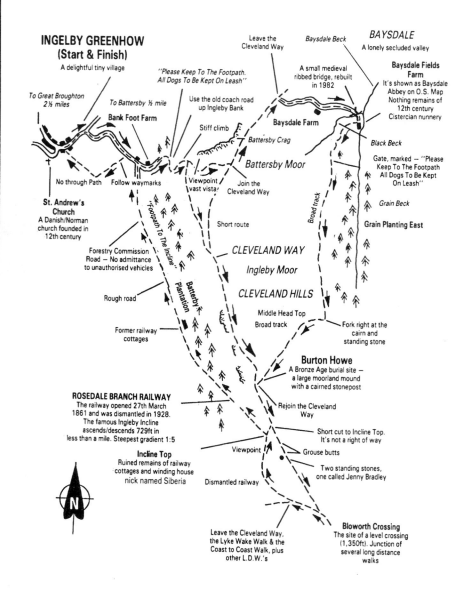

**INGLEBY GREENHOW
(Start & Finish)**
A delightful tiny village

Leave the
Cleveland Way

Baysdale Beck

BAYSDALE
A lonely secluded valley

**Baysdale Fields
Farm**
It's shown as Baysdale
Abbey on O.S. Map
Nothing remains of
12th century
Cistercian nunnery

A small medieval
ribbed bridge, rebuilt
in 1982

*"Please Keep To The Footpath.
All Dogs To Be Kept On Leash"*

To Great Broughton
2½ miles

To Battersby ½ mile

Use the old coach road
up Ingleby Bank

Bank Foot Farm

Stiff climb

Baysdale Farm

Battersby Crag

Black Beck

Gate, marked — "Please
Keep To The Footpath
All Dogs To Be Kept
On Leash"

No through Path

Follow waymarks

Battersby Moor

Viewpoint
vast vista

Join the
Cleveland Way

Grain Beck

Grain Planting East

**St. Andrew's
Church**
A Danish/Norman
church founded in
12th century

"Footpath To The Incline"

Short route

Broad track

CLEVELAND WAY

Ingleby Moor

Forestry Commission
Road — No admittance
to unauthorised vehicles

CLEVELAND HILLS

Rough road

Batterby Plantation

Middle Head Top
Broad track

Former railway
cottages

Fork right at the
cairn and
standing stone

Burton Howe
A Bronze Age burial site —
a large moorland mound
with a cairned stonepost

ROSEDALE BRANCH RAILWAY
The railway opened 27th March
1861 and was dismantled in 1928.
The famous Ingleby Incline
ascends/descends 729ft in
less than a mile. Steepest gradient 1:5

Rejoin the Cleveland
Way

Short cut to Incline Top.
It's not a right of way

Incline Top
Ruined remains of railway
cottages and winding house
nick named Siberia

Viewpoint

Grouse butts

Two standing stones,
one called Jenny Bradley

Dismantled railway

N

Leave the Cleveland Way,
the Lyke Wake Walk & the
Coast to Coast Walk, plus
other L.D.W.'s

Bloworth Crossing
The site of a level crossing
(1,350ft). Junction of
several long distance
walks

5. Ingleby Greenhow

Route: *Ingleby Greenhow — Bank Foot — Ingleby Bank — Baysdale Abbey — Burton Howe — Bloworth Crossing — Ingleby Incline — Bank Foot — Ingleby Greenhow.*
Distance: *Over 7 miles or about 12 moderate miles. Allow 5/6 hours. Moorland tracks with a steep climb.*
O.S. Maps: *Landranger Sheets 93 and 94; Outdoor Leisure Sheet 26.*
Parking: *Limited roadside parking in Ingleby Greenhow.*
Public Transport: *United Services 293 Middlesbrough — Stokesley; rail services — Darlington/Middlesbrough/Battersby Junction. Ingleby Greenhow is half a mile west of Battersby Junction.*
Refreshments: *The Dudley Arms, Ingleby Greenhow.*
Note: *Map and compass needed. Exposed in bad weather. All dogs must be on a leash. When there is a fire danger on these moors do not smoke or light fires.*

This moorland walk is without doubt one of the best in the Cleveland Hills for superb panoramic views.

Start from the lovely little village of Ingleby Greenhow, situated at the foot of the Cleveland Hills and before you set out, take the opportunity to visit the remarkable Danish/Norman Church of St Andrew's, partly rebuilt in 1741. It is a gem of a church and well worth a visit.

Walk along the Battersby road for 440 yards and turn right for a mile to Bank Foot Farm situated below the wooded Cleveland Hills.

Go up past the farm, bear left through the facing gate and follow the rough road (footpath signposted) uphill through Battersby Plantation. The route follows part of the old coach road from Stokesley to Kirkbymoorside for a steep climb of 500 feet, in less than a mile, up Ingleby Bank.

The gated track winds right and left and right again, where a notice requests you to keep to the footpaths and that all dogs should be on a leash. As you climb, note the unfolding views at the top of Ingleby Bank, a popular viewpoint known locally as Turkey Nab although not shown on Ordnance Survey Maps. Admire the extensive views over the Cleveland Plain, including the well-known landmarks of Roseberry Topping and Captain Cook's Monument.

Here you can shorten the walk. Turn sharp right and ascend the old coach road up to the Cleveland Way on Ingleby Moor for 1½ miles southwards above Greenhow Bank to Burton Howe to the join the main moorland walk.

For the longer walk leave the coach road at the same sharp bend and take the cairned moor path on your left (check map, you can easily miss it) which veers left to reach the same broad level sandy track of the Cleveland Way.

Turn left, northwards along this popular route on Battersby Moor for 880 yards and pass through a couple of gates to reach the road. Here you leave the Cleveland Way and turn right down the unfenced road for a mile walk into the lonely secluded valley of beautiful Baysdale.

On the way down pass Baysdale Farm and further on, cross the small medieval bridge (rebuilt in 1982) over the Black Beck, where there is a notice "Private Road" — do not be deterred, the farm

St Andrew's Church, Ingleby Greenhow

road is a right of way. As you approach the large grey farm called Baysdale Fields Farm, shown as Baysdale Abbey on O.S. maps — it stands on the site of the twelfth century Cistercian nunnery, no longer visible — turn right through a faded white-painted gate away to your right.

Follow the faint path through the gated fields (check map) and slant up to a rusty gate by a broken stile below the pine plantation. Go through the gate for a stiff climb up the forest track and out through a white gate, giving access to Ingleby Moor. A notice states "Keep to the footpath and all dogs should be on a leash".

Head southwards along a good track for a ridge walk on the flanks of Middle Head above the wooded valley of Grain Beck. After 1½ miles look out for a standing stone and a cairn on your right, where the heather and burnt moor meet. Fork right, south westwards up the cairned moor for another ridge walk along Middle Head Top with a boundary stone seen up to your right.

Fork left and follow this moorland track for under a mile, to reach the cairned moorland mound of Burton Howe, a Bronze Age burial site.

(Continued on page 16)

15

(Continued from page 15)

Go down to the Cleveland Way, where both walks meet and admire the splendid view of the Cleveland Hills. Turn left for a glorious walk southwards along this long distance footpath, and by a line of grouse butts, there is a short cut, but not a right of way, down to the famous Ingleby Incline.

To carry on with the main walk you will pass a couple of standing stones, the shorter and older one is called Jenny Bradley, while the taller stone is inscribed with "Sir W. Fowles 1838".

Half-a-mile on, you reach Bloworth Crossing (1,350ft), the site of a level crossing where the old Rudland Rigg road joins the old Rosedale railway. This remote spot is a sort of Clapham Junction where several long distance walks meet. Turn right and follow the old railway track shared by the Cleveland Way, the famous Lyke Wake Walk and the Coast to Coast Walk, which in 440 yards, all turn left up to Botton Head.

Keep on the railway track for a mile to reach the ruined remains at Incline Top. This lofty spot was nicknamed Siberia by local railwaymen. Admire the vast vista and go down the famous Ingleby Incline which descends 729 feet in less than a mile with a gradient of 1:5. This single standard gauge railway (second highest in England) opened on March 27, 1861 and was dismantled in 1928.

Enjoy this splendid downhill walk and at the bottom of the incline follow the rough Forestry Commission road for a couple of miles back to Bank Foot.

From here there is a quick return along the same lane used on the outward route or alternatively, follow the way-marked field path walk back to Ingleby Greenhow to end this splendid walk.

A walk through history ...

The Langbaurgh Loop is a new 38 mile challenge walk which takes the serious walker and the rambler through the very best scenery and natural beauty of the area — with many reminders of its long history.

Follow this circular route either for the full distance or in seven easy stages with access to and from the Cleveland Way.

Saltburn
Skinningrove
N. York Moors
Roseberry Topping
The Eston Hills

LANGBAURGH LOOP

T H E
LANGBAURGH
L O O P

A complete guide to the walk is available from Local Tourist Information Centres, price 30p or by post (50p) from:
Tourism & Leisure Dept. LL, Langbaurgh-on-Tees Borough Council, PO Box South Bank 20, Cleveland. TS6 6EL

Langbaurgh
on Tees
BOROUGH COUNCIL

6. Sutton Bank

Route: *Sutton Bank — Garbutt Wood — Southwoods Lodge — Tang Hall — Greendale — Little Moor — Dialstone Farm — Hambleton Inn — Sutton Bank.*
Distance: *Over 7 miles (11km). Allow 3/4 hours. Easy to moderate with a steep, slippery descent and gradual climb up the escarpment.*
O.S.Maps: *Landranger Sheet 100; Outdoor Leisure Sheet 26.*
Parking: *Sutton Bank car park (GR 516831). Do not leave valuables in your car.*
Publications: *Family Walks around Sutton Bank, Sutton Bank Nature Trail, The Hambleton Drove Road — all obtainable from the Sutton Bank Visitor Centre.*
Refreshments: *Cafe, Sutton Bank Visitor Centre; The Hambleton Inn.*
Note: *Do not pick the flowers.*

This high and low level loop follows the popular paths around Sutton Bank for a super seven mile saunter. It offers some of the finest views in England.

From Sutton Bank car park, cross the Cold Kirby road and at the top of Sutton Bank, take the double signposted path "Cleveland Way/Nature Trail Start" on your right. Follow the Sutton Bank Nature Trail shared with the Cleveland Way, and journey northwards along the escarpment edge of Sutton Brow by the pine plantation on your right. See the spectacular views from the high Hambleton Hills across the Vales of Mowbray and York to the distant Yorkshire Dales.

Follow the numbered guide posts of the Nature Trail and at post no.3, turn left diagonally downhill on a sloping path into Garbutt Wood Nature Reserve, managed by the Yorkshire Wildlife Trust. Although the descent is not too difficult, the narrow stony path is fairly steep and slippery.

Continue down through the woodland and pass the huge sandstone boulder called The Boulder Stone (post no.7) and two posts further on, see the small quarry mined for a special soft sandstone called 'Donkey Stone' or 'Hearth Stone'. The trail descends and at post no.10 bear right and do not go down to Lake Gormire. Below post no.13 leave the Nature Trail which doubles back to Sutton Bank. Walk onwards and look up to the 70ft sheer sandstone outcrops of Whitestone Cliff.

Cross a stile, exit out of Garbutt Wood and turn down Thirlby Bank into an enclosed lane to reach Southwoods Lodge, where a public bridleway signpost directs you right along a broad bridleway.

Once through the gate marked "Midge Holme Gate", walk forward over the crossroads (tracks), and keep straight on and as the track bends right uphill in the direction of Southwoods Hall, fork left (check map) on a faint path through the trees and aim through an inset gate (no way-marks or signpost) near a dead tree trunk.

Walk straight on and veer left downhill to go through the far bottom gate by the pine plantation. Go up and at the top of the rise by the young trees in protective plastic sleeves, turn sharp right in front of three hawthorn bushes, and follow the raised route by the line of three transmission poles.

Go through the gate, bear half left down to Tang Hall and turn right to pass the farm on your left.

Turn right, cross the cattle grid and follow the farm road for 880 yards, where at the electro barrier, use the side gate.

At the hillside farm of Greendale with its grazing goats, bear left uphill through a way-marked gate (yellow arrow), and fork right up the hillside to another way-marked gate. Ignore the plastic arrow pointing left and go through the gate and then turn left up by the electric field fence.

Follow the way-marked bridleway (blue arrows) by the walled moorland edge to reach a triple signpost at the junction of three bridle paths. Turn right and take the Little Moor route uphill through the young forestry plantation and at the top cross a stile. Bear half right over the rough moorland pasture, and aim through the way-marked gateposts, near a ruined building.

Go through a gate and follow the bridle track between the wall and plantation. Cross over a forestry drive and continue straight up for a steady climb (very muddy), either by the wall or the plantation.

Both paths bear right and eventually exit through a gate to emerge back onto the Cleveland Way, with extensive escarpment views. Turn right and follow the escarpment edge for a two-mile quick return to Sutton Bank.

Use the same route for the longer walk and in 440 yards, leave the Cleveland Way at the signpost marked "Hambleton Road" by a marooned gate. Turn left and follow the broad bridle track between the fields of growing crops. It is a very muddy walk.

At the road called the Cleveland Road, you have reached the Hambleton Drove Road, the well-known ancient drovers highway. Turn right along this surfaced road, noting the extensive views into Ryedale and over to Roppa Edge with the twin hills of Hawnby and Easterside, both visible.

In half a mile, pass Dialstone Farm which derived its name from the dial or weighing machine used to weigh the jockeys. This farm was once a popular drovers' inn. Beyond the farm at the road junction, cross the road and follow the Hambleton Drove Road southwards on a broad bridle track.

(Continued on page 19)

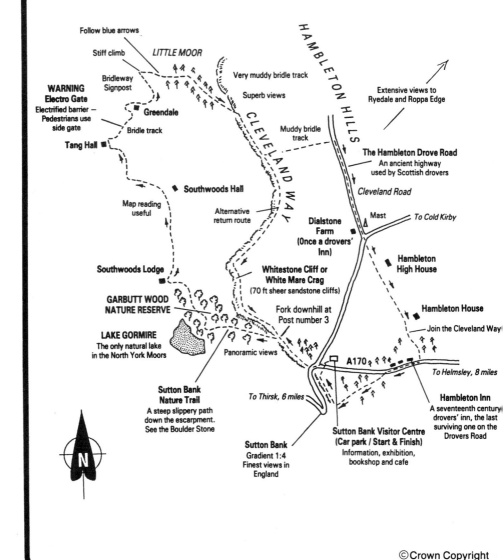

Follow blue arrows

Stiff climb

LITTLE MOOR

Very muddy bridle track

Superb views

**WARNING
Electro Gate**
Electrified barrier —
Pedestrians use
side gate

Bridleway
Signpost

Greendale

Bridle track

Tang Hall

H A M B L E T O N H I L L S

Extensive views to
Ryedale and Roppa Edge

Muddy bridle
track

C L E V E L A N D W A Y

Southwoods Hall

Map reading
useful

Alternative
return route

The Hambleton Drove Road
An ancient highway
used by Scottish drovers

Cleveland Road

**Dialstone
Farm**
**(Once a drovers'
Inn)**

Mast

To Cold Kirby

**Hambleton
High House**

Southwoods Lodge

**Whitestone Cliff or
White Mare Crag**
(70 ft sheer sandstone cliffs)

Hambleton House

— Join the Cleveland Way

**GARBUTT WOOD
NATURE RESERVE**

Fork downhill at
Post number 3

LAKE GORMIRE
The only natural lake
in the North York Moors

Panoramic views

A170

To Helmsley, 8 miles

**Sutton Bank
Nature Trail**
A steep slippery path
down the escarpment.
See the Boulder Stone

To Thirsk, 6 miles

Hambleton Inn
A seventeenth century
drovers' inn, the last
surviving one on the
Drovers Road

Sutton Bank Visitor Centre
(Car park / Start & Finish)
Information, exhibition,
bookshop and cafe

Sutton Bank
Gradient 1:4
Finest views in
England

N

(Continued from page 17)

You will pass High Hambleton House and rejoin the Cleveland Way.

Follow the lane up through Hotel Plantation to come out at the Hambleton Inn — a seventeenth century drovers inn, the last surviving one on the Hambleton Drove Road.

Turn right along the busy A170 and cross the road, when you see the road sign "White Horse Bank". At this T-junction, take the path on your right and follow the Cleveland Way through Kilburn Moor Plantation to come out above Sutton Bank. Turn right and follow the escarpment path for a classic finish of superb views. Return to Sutton Bank car park.

19

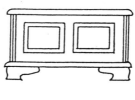
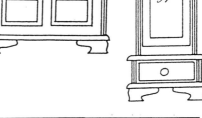

23

25

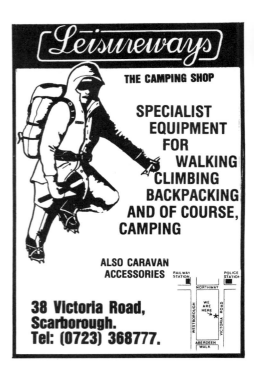
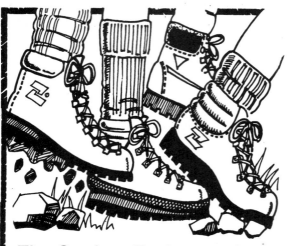

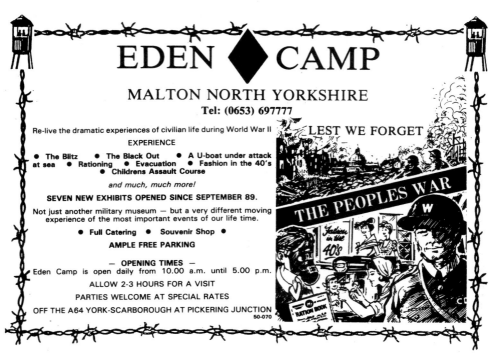

Welcome to the
North York Moors National Park
VISITOR CENTRES

THE MOORS CENTRE, DANBY
The Moors Centre, Danby, Whitby, North Yorkshire, YO21 2NB
Telephone Castleton (0287) 60654

SUTTON BANK
Sutton Bank Information Centre, Sutton Bank, Thirsk
North Yorkshire, YO7 2EK
Telephone (0845) 597426

RAVENSCAR
The National Trust Centre, Ravenscar, Scarborough
Telephone Scarborough (0723) 870138

ROBIN HOOD'S BAY
The Exhibition Centre, Chapel Street, Robin Hood's Bay
Whitby, North Yorkshire
Telephone (0947) 880512

RYEDALE FOLK MUSEUM
Ryedale Folk Museum Information Centre, Hutton-le-Hole
York, North Yorkshire, YO6 6UA
Telephone Lastingham (0515) 367

HELMSLEY
Town Hall, Market Place, Helmsley, North Yorkshire, YO6 5DL
Telephone Helmsley (0439) 70173

*Explore the National Park with the "North York Moors Visitor" newspaper
Price 30p*
*Available from Visitor and Information Centres which also stock a wide range of Trails, Guides
and Walk leaflets*

50-260

Aysgarth Falls seen from Yore Bridge (Walk 16, p61).

Impressive Whitby Abbey (Walk 1, p6).

7. Reeth

Route: *Reeth — Arkle Town or Langthwaite — The White House — Bouldershaw House — Fore Gill Gate — Cringley Hill — Skelgate Lane — Reeth.*
Distance: *Over 8 miles (13km). Allow 4 to 5 hours. Moderate. Field and moorland paths with one stiff climb. Exposed in bad weather.*
O.S. Maps: *Landranger Sheets 98 and 92; Outdoor Leisure Sheet 30.*
Parking: *Park on the cobbled area of The Green, Reeth.*
Public Transport: *United Services 30, Richmond to Keld. Infrequent service. No Sunday service. Check timetables.*
Refreshments: *Pubs and cafes in Reeth; The Red Lion Inn, Langthwaite.*
Note: *A very watery walk. Expect plenty of mud.*

This Reeth ramble is a classic circuit for Herriot fans. Anyone who walks this route will easily recognise Langthwaite Bridge and the Watersplash from the popular TV series, All Creatures Great and Small.

From Reeth follow the Langthwaite road north for 880 yards and beyond the cattle grid, start the walk from a way-marked stile signposted "Langthwaite," left of the house called Sleights Brow. The three-mile meadowland outward route along the west side of Arkengarthdale is well way-marked with yellow painted blobs and arrows on stiles, walls, telegraph poles and boulders. Although it is fairly easy to follow, the most demanding aspect is negotiating stile after stile, plus it is a watery walk with plenty of mud.

In the first half mile, go through at least nine stiles and en route look out for the double footpath sign "Langthwaite/Reeth" wedged in a tree. You can easily miss it. Once through a facing gate, the path meets a farm track and be careful not to go down to the footbridge, but cross over the track and aim for a way-marked stile. On the way, there are good views of the sober hamlet of Booze and the impressive scarred Fremington Edge.

Half a mile further on, the path hugs the way-marked wall on your right and this is the worst part of the walk with mud oozing over the boot tops. Aim through a little red railed gate, cross a stream and pass in front of the fenced farm called West Raw Croft. Follow the way-mark arrows, cross over the farm road and at the far end of the field, go through a way-marked open gateway. Continue on through another open gateway and keep an eye open for the faint path that forks half left uphill to a hidden footpath signpost. You can easily miss this.

Turn right at the signpost and along the same field, exit through a way-marked stile. Half a dozen stiles further on, the path leads down to the Arkle Beck for a pleasant walk upstream. Watch out for the Fore Gill Beck, especially in flood, as there is no footbridge or stepping stones. Wade across this and straddle the step board stile to reach the railed footbridge over the Arkle Beck.

Here you have a choice. Go uphill via the old graveyard with gravestones at all angles (the first church was built in 1145, demolished in 1818 and rebuilt in Langthwaite) into the hamlet of Arkle Town or cross the footbridge and turn left along the bridle track by the Arkle Beck to reach the lovely little village of Langthwaite, regarded as the capital of Arkengarthdale.

It is well-known for its ancient bridge featured in the TV series All Creatures Great and Small, as well as the seventeenth century Red Lion Inn, one of Britain's most-televised pubs — used for Walt Disney's film Escape from the Dark, the ITV series Andy Robson and the film A Woman of Substance.

Leave Langthwaite, cross the ancient bridge and road walk to Arkle Town, where at the sign "The White House" turn right up the stony track. It is signposted "Bridleway" and pass the whitewashed White House on your right. Go through the gate and follow the track, walled at first, out on to the open moor. Follow the track for a steady but stiff climb of some 400 feet up past Gill House, where the track deteriorates to become a boggy path.

As you climb admire the retrospective views of Arkengarthdale dominated by Fremington Edge and Calver Hill. Aim through a wooden gate and continue up the trackless moor and, by the barn buildings of Bouldershaw House, turn right along the farm track to the Langthwaite — Low Row road and by the "Eggs for Sale" sign, turn left along the open moor road, giving fine views to Swaledale and back to Arkengarthdale.

Follow this elevated road for 880 yards noting the surrounding lead mining landscapes. When you see the road signs "Z Bend" and "1:5" look down on Fore Gill Gate, better known as the Watersplash used in the opening of the TV series All Creatures Great and Small. This well-known spot is a popular picnic place during the summer.

At the top of the "Z Bend" fork left through the wooden gate signposted "Bridleway Only, No Vehicles" and follow the track on to Reeth Low Moor. Keep by the wall on your right and where the track turns left, bear half right and follow a faint track at first, through the heather, which skirts the flanks of Cringley Hill. Descend the track and aim by the wire-fenced enclosure on your right and further on, pass below a three field walled enclosure which is on your left.

(Continued on page 37)

7. Reeth

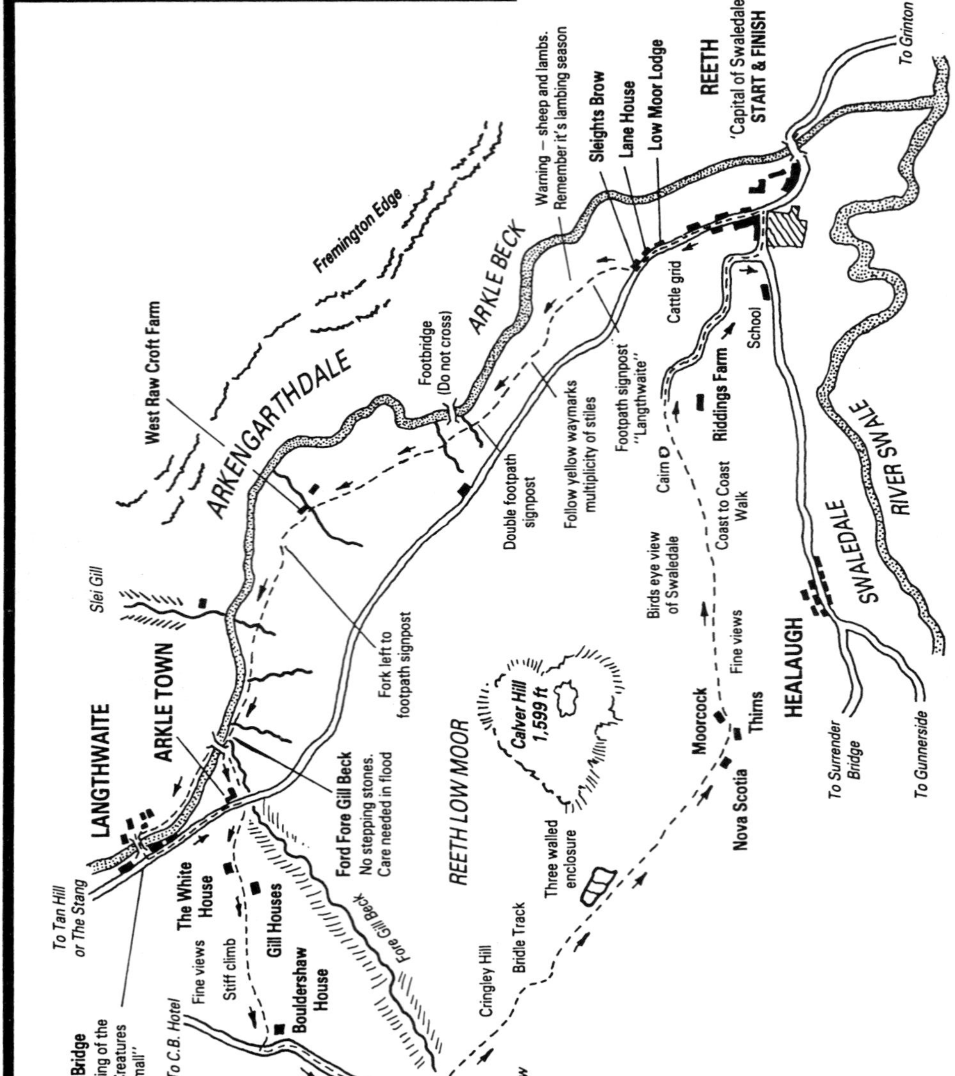

To Grinton

REEH
'Capital of Swaledale'
START & FINISH

Warning — sheep and lambs.
Remember it's lambing season

Sleights Brow
Lane House
Low Moor Lodge

ARKLE BECK

Cattle grid

School

Footpath signpost
"Langthwaite"

Riddings Farm

Follow yellow waymarks
multiplicity of stiles

Cairn ⊕

Coast to Coast
Walk

Birds eye view
of Swaledale

Moorcock

Fine views

Thirns

HEALAUGH

Nova Scotia

SWALEDALE

RIVER SWALE

To Surrender Bridge

To Gunnerside

Footbridge
(Do not cross)

Double footpath
signpost

ARKENGARTHDALE

West Raw Croft Farm

Fremington Edge

Slei Gill

Fork left to
footpath signpost

Calver Hill
1,599 ft

REETH LOW MOOR

Three walled
enclosure

Bridle Track

Cringley Hill

To Low Row

LANGTHWAITE

ARKLE TOWN

Ford Fore Gill Beck
No stepping stones.
Care needed in flood

Fore Gill Beck

To Tan Hill
or The Stang

The White House

Fine views

Stiff climb

Gill Houses

Bouldershaw House

To C.B. Hotel

Langthwaite Bridge
Used in the opening of the
TV series "All Creatures
Great and Small"

Fore Gill Gate
Better known as
"The Watersplash"
used in the opening
of the TV series
"All Creatures Great
and Small"

N

© **Crown Copyright**

(Continued from page 35)

Here check the map, as the right of way forks right to a parallel track — the Coast to Coast Walk, which leads you down by the farmsteads of Nova Scotia, Thirns and up by Moorcock House back to the moor route. Alternatively, from the walled enclosure, you can walk straight on eastwards along a good track which eventually joins the Coast to Coast Walk. Follow this open moor route, then hug the intake wall on your right with the rounded summit of Calver Hill (1,599ft) away up to your left. You can see Healaugh below, with Harkerside (1,676ft) and its ancient Maiden Castle across the valley.

Cross another open stretch of moor, aim for a cairn with Riddings Farm seen below and go through a corner gate into the walled Skelgate Lane, giving a bird's eye view of Swaledale. Go down the lane, which is very watery and muddy, to exit out on to the B6270. Turn left down School Bank to complete the circuit back to Reeth.

8. Gunnerside

N

Join the Coast to Coast Walk

OLD GANG MINES
Extensive old spoil tips and re-worked spoils

COAST TO COAST WALK

Grouse Butts

BUNTON LEVEL
Extensive dressing floors, water wheel pit and roofless buildings.

MELBECKS MOOR

Swine Bank Scar

Cairns

Bunton Hush

North Hush

LOWNATHWAITE LEAD MINES

Batcher Gill

Waterfall

Sir Francis Dressing Floors
'Do not climb on wall on historic buildings.'

Sir Francis Level
Level entrance water wheel pit, dressing floors started in 1864

GUNNERSIDE
A former lead mining centre named after 'Gunmar' – a Viking chieftain
(Start & Finish)

Gunnerside Beck

Birbeck Wood

Woodland Walk or use parallel field path

GUNNERSIDE GILL

To Calvert Houses

To Muker
3 miles

RIVER SWALE

B6270

B6270

To Reeth – 6 miles

Follow yellow waymarks

Metal Gate Please Close The Gate

Viewpoint
Excellent views of Upper Swaledale

Heights

Barf Side

BLADES
A tiny hamlet.
John Wesley made his first visit in 1761 and his last in 1780

BROWNSEY MOOR

Feetham Pasture

To Smarber

Join the Corpse Way in reverse

To Low Row

Viewpoint
Magnificent views of Calver Hill, Harkerside and Marrick Priory

To Fleetham

Follow the Swaledale Marathon in reverse

Surrender Bridge

To Healaugh

Grouse Butt No. 4

Cattle Grid

To Langthwaite

Mill Gill or Old Gang Beck

Leave the Coast to Coast Walk

OLD GANG LEAD SMELTING MILL
This Scheduled Ancient Monument is being conserved. Please do not clamber on walls or cause any damage Y.D.N.P.

Peat Store
390 feet in length and 21 feet in width

Level House Bridge

Site of dressing floor

Hard Level Gill

Flincher Gill

8. Gunnerside

Route: *Gunnerside — Bunton Level — Level House Bridge — Surrender Bridge — Blades — Gunnerside.*
Distance: *Over 9 miles (14.5km). Allow 5/6 hours. Moderate. A high-level moorland walk exposed in bad weather with a very steep climb.*
O.S. Maps: *Landranger Sheets 98 and 92 or 91; Outdoor Leisure 30.*
Parking: *Limited parking in Gunnerside between the Literary Institute (1877) and Little Bridge (1911) west of Gunnerside Beck.*
Public Transport: *United Service 30 from Richmond. Check timetable.*
Refreshments: *The King's Head, bar meals; Ghyllfoot, morning coffee, lunches and afternoon teas. (Sorry, no dogs allowed.)*
Warning: *Do not explore mines and keep out of the shaft levels and old flues.*

This moorland walk follows the old miners tracks, known as 'Gruvers Trods', around some of the best uplands ways of Swaledale and highlights the bygone world of the lead mining industry.

Leave Gunnerside by the sign "Footpath to Gunnerside Gill", between Little Bridge and Troutbeck House, opposite the King's Head. Follow the beckside path northwards, turn right in front of a white gate, climb eight steps ("Gunnerside Gill" sign) and pass through a gate marked "Please Shut The Gate". Turn left, pass behind Gunnarsgill Hall, a former Methodist day school, now a private residence, and follow the yellow waymarks onwards through a small gate to the wooded beckside path.

Walk upstream with care, noting the large boulders and flood embankment, to exit through a small gate on your right. Here you have a choice of paths, both join further on. Uphill there is a waymarked pasture path parallel to my route.

Turn left, climb the steps and follow the sign "Woodland Path" up through Burbeck Wood for a muddy high-level woodland walk. Within the wood, a waymarked tree stump directs you down and out of the wood via a stile into the valley bottom.

Follow the yellow waymarks through further stiles (joined by the parallel pasture path) to reach the first lead mining ruins in Gunnerside Gill, about two miles north from Gunnerside. Do not climb the walls of the dressing floors of the Old Gang Mining Company. Beyond the ruins, cross the corner fence stile, bear right up the bracken path and turn left along a level path, a former mine tramway by the wall on your right.

Continue and cross a stile in the wall, with no more stiles on the entire walk. Climb up the 'Gruvers Trod' and follow in the footsteps of the 'gruvers' who knitted as they walked to the T'Owd Man, meaning mines, and enjoyed 'six needles', a favourite expression for a rest.

The track levels out below the outcrops of Swina Bank Scar, opposite Botcher Gill with its waterfall. After a mile you reach Bunton Level in the heart of Swaledale's industrial past — a dramatic lead mining landscape ravaged by the man-made hushes of Bunton, Friarfold, Gorton and North. Despite the desecration, the hushes and mines are impressive on the purple heathery hillside. Do not explore Bunton Level or its waterwheel pit or derelict buildings — they are dangerous.

About 200 yards beyond Bunton Level, join the Coast to Coast Walk and turn right by a cairn and follow the green track to Bunton Hush, directly above Bunton Level, where you turn left up the man-made hush for a steep scramble and boulder-hopping exercise.

Near the top of the Y-shaped hush, fork left up the tongue for a further climb on to Melbecks Moor (check map). Head eastwards for a small cairn on this desolate moor top (1,863ft) and aim for two more cairns to reach a broad track traversing east through a desert wasteland of extensive old spoil heaps and re-worked spoils.

Follow the track eastwards for 1½ miles down the moor to cross Level House Bridge, where you turn right through a gate and follow the old miners' track by Hard Level Gill for about a mile to reach the extensive ruins of the Old Gang smelting mill.

Beyond the smelt mill, follow the track for 1½ miles to reach the Langthwaite/Low Row road, turn right and cross Surrender Bridge over Old Gang Beck. Follow this road uphill and opposite no.4 grouse butt, bear right along the green track traversing south west over Feetham Pasture for a further mile to enter the tiny hamlet of Blades. Leave Blades and walk westwards along the elevated road, giving superb views of Swaledale.

After 880 yards, this cul-de-sac road turns down to Smarber, but my route continues straight on and follows the green track westwards, first by the wall and then along the escarpment known as The Barf (1,250ft).

Once through the metal gate marked "Please Close The Gate", turn immediately left down the winding green track for a mile to pass by Heights and back to Gunnerside.

39

EASBY ABBEY
Extensive ruins, founded for the white-robed Premonstratensian canon's in about 1155, by Roald, Constable of Richmond Castle.

ABBEY MILL
A former water corn mill, now kennels and cattery. (Dogs must be on lead.)

DANGER
Riverbank liable to erosion and undercutting.

Easby Parish Church dedicated to St. Agatha of Sicily

Car Park

Abbey House

ABBEY WOOD

NOTICE – ABBEY WOOD
Public Footpaths Only. No Entry for Vehicles or Horses except for access to Red House Farm. Dogs must be on Lead. Please keep to footpaths. N.Y.C.C.

NOTICE
Public Footpath.
Dogs mist be on leads.
Please keep to footpaths. N.Y.C.C.

Sewage Works

Views to Easby Abbey

IRON BRIDGE
Old railway bridge over the River Swale.

Steps and Stile

Low Path

Backhouse Ings

Top Path

Disused Railway Line

THE DRUMMER BOY STONE

Clint Bank Wood

Lombards Wynd

Easby Low Road

A6136

To Catterick

St. Mary's Church

Station Road

Frenchgate

School

BATTS

MERCURY BRIDGE
Station Bridge renamed Mercury Bridge to commemorate the Royal Corps Signals in Catterick on 11th July 1975. Built in 1848.

Waterfalls

RIVER SWALE

Market Place

Castle

RICHMOND

RICHMONDSHIRE MUSEUM
Ryder's Wynd
Local History and 'Herriot' Vets' surgery.

Start & Finish

N

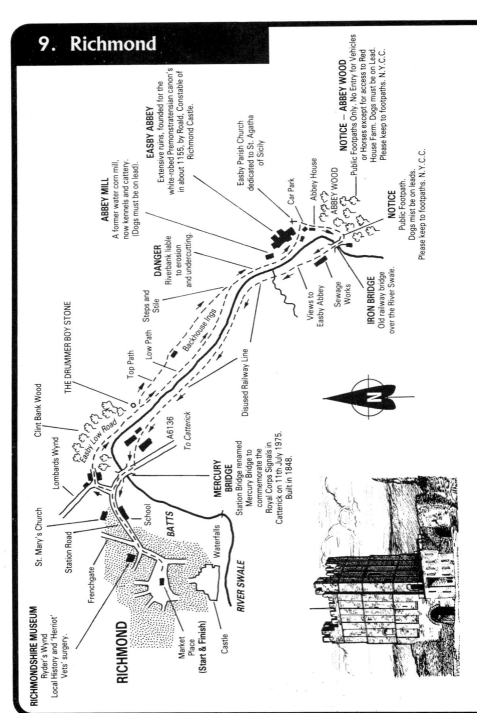

9. Richmond

Route: *Richmond — Clink Bank Wood — Easby Abbey — Iron Bridge — Mercury Bridge — Richmond.*
Distance: *3 miles (4.8km). Easy. Allow 2/3 hours.*
O.S. Maps: *Landranger Sheets 92 & 99; 1:25,000 Sheets NZ 10 & SE19.*
Parking: *Market Place, Richmond (disc parking, maximum 2 hours); Nuns Close Car Park, Hurgill Road, Richmond.*
Public Transport: *United Services from Darlington, Catterick, Hawes and Keld.*
Refreshments: *Plenty of pubs, hotels and cafes in Richmond.*

Here is a gentle three-miler and every one a good mile from the historic market town of Richmond in Swaledale.

This pleasant riverside ramble, with a return along an old railway track, is one of the finest walks around Richmond, and provides an ideal introduction to Swaledale. It is a walk for all seasons and suitable for almost everyone.

Leave Richmond at the bottom of the cobbled Market Place, turn left by the shop called Richmond Lady.

Walk down to the A6163, unless you decide to visit Richmondshire Museum*, up Ryders Wynd, to see the wide range of local history exhibits, the reconstructed Cruck House and the James Herriot surgery set from the BBC TV series All Creatures Great and Small. It is well worth the diversion.

By Swale House, turn right down Station Road (A6163) and pass St Mary's Church, restored about 1860 by Sir Giles Gilbert Scott. Beyond the church, turn left along the short walled lane and then right at the junction of Lombards Wynd and Easy Low Road, the latter, an ancient route used by the white robed canons to Easby Abbey.

Follow this ancient way, an unsurfaced lane, signposted "Easby Abbey" up into Clink Bank Wood along a tree-lined track, giving some of the best views of the River Swale and Richmond. Below Clink Banks, the popular path divides into the Top Path and the Low Path.

At the approach to the Top Path look for the upright slab stone wedged behind the gatepost of a padlocked gate, to see the Drummer Boy Stone, erected to mark the last known spot, where the drummer boy was heard as he drummed and explored underground passages reputed to exist between Richmond Castle and Easby Abbey!

Turn right and follow the Low Path along Backhouse Ings for a riverside ramble, with some mud in places. After 880 yards, leave the wooded riverside, climb up the single railed 20 steps and cross the way-marked stile into the field, with your first glimpse of Easby Abbey seen ahead. Turn right along the field, pass a couple of notices stating "Danger — Riverbank liable to erosion and undercutting" to cross the corner way-marked stile by Abbey Mill Kennel and Cattery, with a notice saying "Footpath users are requested to keep dogs on a lead". Turn left by Abbey Mill, a former water corn mill and continue straight ahead along the surfaced private road to Easby Abbey. The land by the river is private property and not a public right of way.

The secluded monastic ruins beautifully situated near the River Swale, were immortalised in water colours by Joseph W. Turner, and are regarded as the most picturesque in North Yorkshire. The Abbey of St Agatha at Easby was founded by Roald, Constable of Richmond Castle about 1155 for the white canons of the Presmonstratensian Order. There is an admission charge. Easby Church, next to the abbey, dedicated also to St Agatha is older than the abbey, although the exact date is unknown. Both the abbey and church are well worth a visit.

From the church, pass the cobbled car park, turn right, pass Abbey House and cross a stile by a green gate. Follow the riverside lane up into Abbey Wood with a notice stating "Public Footpaths Only, Dogs must be on a lead. Please keep to footpaths". When you see a similar notice, turn right over Iron Bridge, the old railway bridge across the Swale to reach the disused railway line — the Richmond railway line from Eryholme Junction, opened on September 10, 1901 and closed March 3, 1969.

Converted into a country walk, follow the rail track bed straight on for under a mile. Apart from the smell from nearby sewage works, this is a delightful return, with excellent views to Easby Abbey.

When you reach the old railway terminus, pass between Richmond Swimming Pool and Richmond Garden and Farm Supply centre, housed in the former Richmond Station. Turn right along the A6163, cross Mercury Bridge (the former Station Bridge built in 1846) and up Station Road back to the Market Place.

* *The museum is open daily between April 1 to October 31, 11am to 5pm. There is an admission charge.*

N

NOTICE – RICHMOND OLD RACECOURSE

1. Pedestrians are requested to use the public footpaths and not trespass on the horse gallops.

2. No dogs allowed except on a leash or under strict control.

By Order of Burgage Pastures Committee

See the old stone Race Judges Box (erected A.D. 1814. W. S. Goodburn Esq., Mayor)

OLD RICHMOND RACECOURSE

RICHMOND
A picturesque and historic market town – Gateway to Swaledale

Racecourse Road

Nuns Close Car Park (Start & Finish)

Quarry Road

Gallowfields Trading Estate

Reeth Road

High Gingerfield Lodge

Westfields

Whitcliffe Farm

A6108

RIVER SWALE

Aske Beck

Jockey Cap Clump

RICHMOND BEACON On Beacon Hill, 1,045ft. above sea level

Beacon Lane

Coalsgarth Gate

Coalsgarth Edge

Ford

Beacon Hill

Beacon Cottage

Beacon Plantation

Old Reeth Road

VIEWPOINT Fine panoramic views

High Leases

Whitcliffe Wood

SWALEDALE

To Reeth

Lownethwaite Bridge

Waymarked post with blue arrow

Look for two tall yellow waymark posts

RICHMOND OUT MOOR

Twin radio masts

Stile

Whitcliffe Scar

To Marske

WILLANCE'S LEAP 1606

Two monuments erected to commemorate Robert Willance's leap, when he galloped his horse over Whitcliffe Scar and survived

10. Richmond

Route: *Richmond — Old Racecourse — Beacon Lane — Richmond Out Moor — Willance's Leap — Westfields — Richmond.*
Distance: *6 miles (9.5km). Allow 3 hours. Easy to moderate with some climbs. Field, moorland paths, lanes and roads.*
O.S. Maps: *Landranger Sheet 92; 1:25,000 Sheet NZ 10.*
Parking: *Nuns Close Car Park, off Hurgill Road, Richmond (270 spaces).*
Public Transport: *Richmond is served by United Services from Darlington, Catterick, Hawes and Keld.*
Refreshments: *Plenty of pubs, hotels and cafes in Richmond. None on route.*
Note: *On Old Richmond Racecourse — "Please keep off the gallops" and "All dogs must be on a lead" — Richmond Burgage Lands.*

Six of the best miles around Richmond reward this airy upland walk with fine views and include the well-known landmarks of Richmond Beacon and Willance's Leap.

Start from Nuns Close car park in Richmond. Turn left up Hurgill Road and right into Quarry Road for a steep climb northwards out of Richmond, with grand backward views of this historic town. At the road junction, go straight up Racecourse Road and at the top of Gallowfields Industrial Estate, where the road bends left, go across the road to the public footpath signpost, right of M. J. Fenwick (Plumbing & Heating).

Follow the path and cross the stone wall stile to come out onto the old Richmond Racecourse. Turn left, walk westwards and pass the old stone Race Judges Box (erected 1814), where beyond, go through a white gate to the road.

Turn right along the Old Reeth Road (no footway — take care), pass High Gingerfield Lodge and in 880 yards, turn right by Beacon Cottage to enter the unsignposted Beacon Lane. Follow this enclosed lane for two miles along Coalsgarth Edge, giving good views over the Aske Estates.

On the way, you will see up to your left Richmond Beacon on Beacon Hill (1045ft) — an ancient signal station lit during the Spanish Armada. Although my route bypasses this lofty spot, walkers should check the O. S. map, as there is a public right of way up to the Beacon.

The lane leads down to the ford crossing of the Aske Beck at Coalsgarth Gate, where you must negotiate the step stones, as well as the facing wooden gate. From the ford, climb up the track for 440 yards to a metal gate with blue waymark arrows. Do not go through the gate, but follow the path by the left-hand side of the gate to a white way-marked post with blue arrows. Turn left and follow the path southwards over Richmond Out Moor planted with young trees and noting the twin radio masts on the horizon. Cross Aske Beck and a couple of tall metal waymark posts, erected by the Ramblers' Association, direct you up the moor by Beacon Plantation to exit through a gate to the Old Reeth Road.

Turn right along the road for about 50 yards and opposite, a public footpath sign directs you over a ladder stile in the wall. Turn half right, follow the path which merges with a tractor track for a short distance, then shoot southwards down the rough pasture, aiming for the top of the monument peeping out above the wall.

Go through the small gate to the double inscribed monuments known as Willance's Leap. In 1606, Robert Willance while hunting in bad weather, miraculously escaped death after his mare took three leaps, each over 24 feet and plunged 200 feet over Whitcliffe Scar. The horse was killed and Willance survived. On this fatal spot, he erected three memorial stones 24 feet apart, although only two remain today.

There are splendid views down Swaledale and even Pen Hill and Great Whernside are both visible. Turn left, eastwards along the escarpment of Whitcliffe Scar for a mile and en route cross a low wall and straddle a fence. Continue along field fenced path above Whitcliffe Wood and veer left above the gorse bushes to go through an open gateway in the facing fence. Pause here to admire the extensive views eastwards over Richmond and across the Vale of Mowbray to the Cleveland Hills.

Follow the track straight on and curve right down the hillside to come out opposite High Leases Farm. Turn left along the gated farm track, pass the white-washed Whitcliffe Farm and follow the surfaced road down Westfields for a mile return to Richmond.

11. Cray

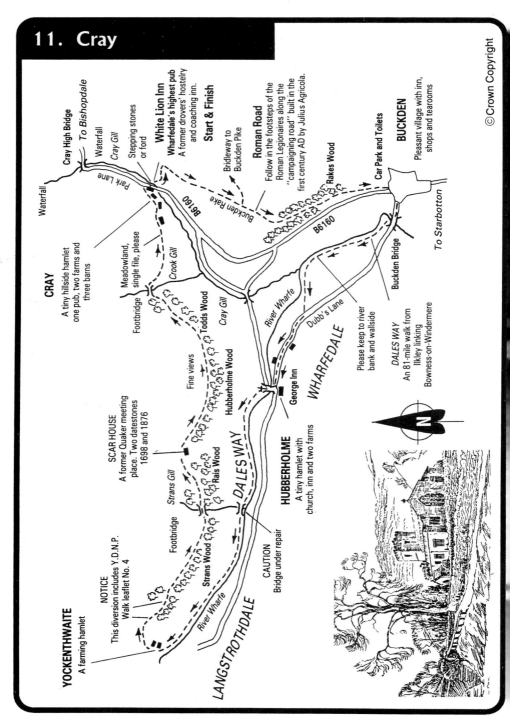

Cray High Bridge

Waterfall

To Bishopdale

Waterfall

Cray Gill

Stepping stones or ford

White Lion Inn
Wharfedale's highest pub
A former drovers' hostelry and coaching inn.

Start & Finish

Bridleway to Buckden Pike

Roman Road
Follow in the footsteps of the Roman Legionaires along the "campaigning road" built in the first century AD by Julius Agricola.

Rakes Wood

BUCKDEN
Pleasant village with inn, shops and tearooms

Waterfall

Park Lane

B6160

Buckden Rake

CRAY
A tiny hillside hamlet one pub, two farms and three barns

Meadowland, single file, please

Crook Gill

Footbridge

Todds Wood

Cray Gill

B6160

Car Park and Toilets

Buckden Bridge

To Starbotton

Fine views

Hubberholme Wood

River Wharfe

George Inn

Dubb's Lane

WHARFEDALE

Please keep to river bank and wallside

DALES WAY
An 81-mile walk from Ilkley linking Bowness-on-Windermere

SCAR HOUSE
A former Quaker meeting place. Two datestones 1698 and 1876

Strans Gill

Rais Wood

DALES WAY

HUBBERHOLME
A tiny hamlet with church, inn and two farms

Footbridge

Strans Wood

CAUTION
Bridge under repair

YOCKENTHWAITE
A farming hamlet

NOTICE
This diversion includes Y.D.N.P. Walk leaflet No. 4

River Wharfe

LANGSTROTHDALE

N

11. Cray

Route: *Cray — Buckden — Hubberholme — Yockenthwaite — Cray.*
Distance: *6.8 miles (11km). Easy. Allow 3/4 hours. Couple of climbs.*
O.S. Maps: *Landranger Sheet 98; Outdoor Leisure 30.*
Parking: *Customer car park, White Lion Inn, Cray.*
Refreshments: *White Lion Inn, Cray; Buck Inn also tea rooms in Buckden; George Inn, Hubberholme.*

Try this eternal triangle, which is a gem of a ramble from the White Lion Inn at Cray — Wharfedale's highest pub — and explore The Valley of the Bucks, better known as Upper Wharfedale and Langstrothdale.

From Cray, opposite the pub, cross Cray Gill and follow the signposted path uphill for a stiff climb to Buckden Rake. At the top, turn right through a gate signposted "Buckden" and stride out along the old Roman road for over a mile, following in the footsteps of the Romans. There are fine views over Wharfedale and up Langstrothdale.

Continue southwards down through Rakes Wood into the picturesque village of Buckden, which housed the foresters of Langstrothdale Chase in medieval times.

Leave Buckden by Dubbs Lane, and beyond Buckden Bridge (known as Election Bridge), turn right through a gate signposted "Hubberholme — 1 mile". The walk now follows the Dales Way along by the River Wharfe with detailed direction not needed, although you are requested to keep by the river bank and wallside. Rejoin Dubbs Lane and follow it to the tiny hamlet of Hubberholme, named after the Viking Chief Hubba.

The George Inn hosts the Hubberholme Parliament held on New Year's Day, and maintains the 1,000-year annual land-letting custom. Across the bridge is the lovely little church of St. Michael and All Angels, a popular pilgrimage for most visitors. This ancient church boasts a famous rood loft (1558) and pews made by the 'mouse man', Robert Thompson of Kilburn. Find the 'Mouse' trademark.

Behind the churchyard, follow the Dales Way along Langstrothdale for 1½ miles to Yockenthwaite. It is a lovely riverside ramble — well way-marked, stiled and signposted. As you approach the farming hamlet of Yockenthwaite (Yocket), bear right up to a corner wall stile, cross this and pass the sheep pens; go through a gate, turn right up the farm track and leave the Dales Way. Pass the farm on your right and a couple of footpath signs direct you up the fellside track for a stiff, stony climb, with unfolding views across the valley to Horse Head Moor. Near the top, cross a

The White Lion, Cray

signposted ladder stile into Strans Wood and follow the diversion signposts which lead you up and out of the wood on to the limestone pavement above.

Head eastwards along this high level route above Strans Wood with good views. Follow the yellow way-marks through a series of small fields with broken walls, gaps and way-marked stiles. Over a mile, veer left up to a metal footbridge which spans the narrow chasm of Strans Gill. Walk through Rais Wood and further on, pass behind Scar House, where a triple signpost points eastwards to Cray. Keep on the level limestone shelf above Hubberholme Wood and look for a concealed way-marked stile in the wall. There are splendid views across Cray Valley to Buckden Pike, and down Wharfedale to Buckden Village and beyond.

After another mile, cross the wooden footbridge over Crook Gill and proceed eastwards over a couple of meadowlands (single file), pass by some barns and finish back at the hillside hamlet of Cray, where a warm welcome awaits you at the White Lion Inn.

This cosy country pub, a former drovers hostlery offers real ales from Goose Eye and Youngers, and home-cooked bar meals in the stone-flagged bar, where you can try your hand at Ring the Bull — stand-up indoor quoits.

East Stonesdale Farm

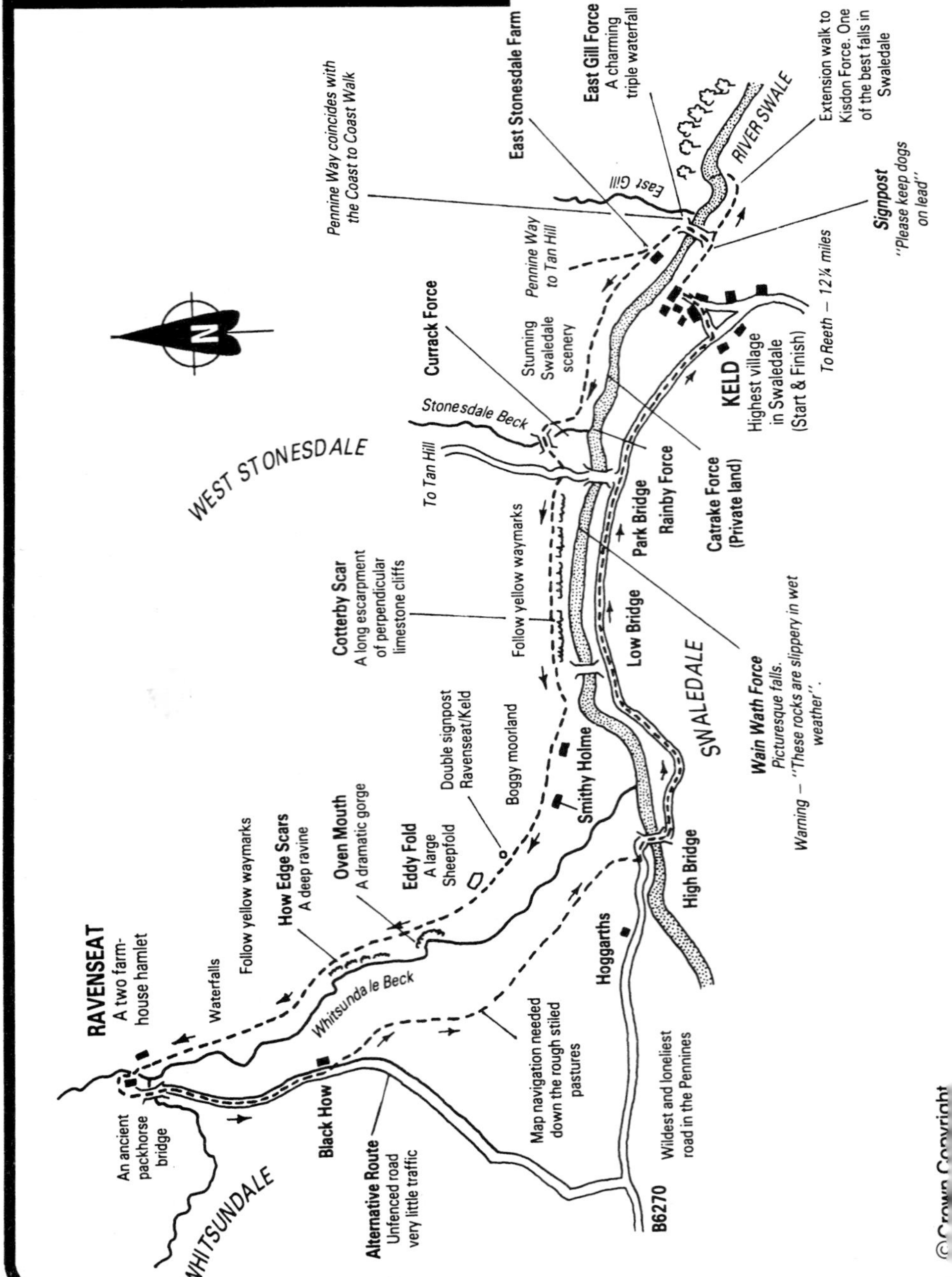

East Gill Force
A charming triple waterfall

Extension walk to Kisdon Force. One of the best falls in Swaledale

Pennine Way coincides with the Coast to Coast Walk

East Gill

RIVER SWALE

Pennine Way to Tan Hill

Signpost
"Please keep dogs on lead"

To Reeth — 12¼ miles

Currack Force

Stunning Swaledale scenery

KELD
Highest village in Swaledale (Start & Finish)

Stonesdale Beck

To Tan Hill

WEST STONESDALE

Park Bridge

Rainby Force

Catrake Force
(Private land)

Cotterby Scar
A long escarpment of perpendicular limestone cliffs

Follow yellow waymarks

Low Bridge

SWALEDALE

Wain Wath Force
Picturesque falls.

Warning — "These rocks are slippery in wet weather".

Double signpost Ravenseat/Keld

Boggy moorland

Smithy Holme

Eddy Fold
A large Sheepfold

How Edge Scars
A deep ravine

Oven Mouth
A dramatic gorge

Follow yellow waymarks

Waterfalls

High Bridge

RAVENSEAT
A two farm-house hamlet

Whitsunda le Beck

Hoggarths

Map navigation needed down the rough stiled pastures

Wildest and loneliest road in the Pennines

B6270

An ancient packhorse bridge

Black How

Alternative Route
Unfenced road very little traffic

WHITSUNDALE

N

12. Keld

Route: *Keld — Smithy Holme — Ravenseat — High Bridge — Keld*
Distance: *6 miles (10km). Easy to moderate. Allow 3½—4 hours. Field and fell footpaths. Some road walking.*
O.S. Maps: *Landranger Sheet 98; Outdoor Leisure Sheet 30; Stile Publications Upper Swaledale Footpath Map and Guide recommended.*
Parking: *Lower end of Keld village. Farm access, please keep clear. Do not obstruct gateways.*
Public Transport: *United Services 30, Richmond to Keld. Infrequent service, check timetables.*

Save this walk for a wet day when the many waterfalls around Keld in Upper Swaledale are much more impressive after rain and the rumble, tumble of water can be heard everywhere.

At the bottom of Keld village, leave by the signpost "Public Footpath to Muker" and follow Keld Lane along the Pennine Way. After 400 yards at the double Pennine Way sign fork left downhill to cross the footbridge over the River Swale. Go up the path near the three levels of East Gill Force, the first of half a dozen waterfalls on this walk.

Above the falls the Pennine Way coincides with the Coast to Coast Walk. Turn left along the track (signposted "East Stonesdale Farm") for a stiff uphill climb to the farm where the Pennine Way heads north for Tan Hill. Turn left above the farm, using the Coast to Coast Walk along the elevated broad bridleway for 880 yards, giving glimpses of a couple of waterfalls, Catrake Force and Currack Force, in stunning Swaledale scenery.

At the road hairpin bend, turn right and almost opposite, go through the gate with a footpath sign fixed to the gatepost. Walk westwards along Cotterby Scar, a long escarpment of 1,000 yards with perpendicular limestone cliffs. Follow the yellow way-marks through wall gaps and over stiles, with fine views of Wain Wath Force, better seen on the return road route.

At the end of the scar, turn right up the gated track, pass a farm and onwards through the gate marked "Smithy Holme Farm", follow the track to the empty farm of Smithy Holme. Here turn half left, pass a Land-Rover without wheels, and traverse the rough open wet moor. Aim for the double signpost "Ravenseat/Keld" and pass Eddy Fold, awarded an Oscar by Alfred Wainwright for being the biggest sheep fold ever seen. Continue onwards following the footpath markers, yellow blobs of paint, along the gated pastures with waymarked barns. Peep over the wall and see the dramatic ravine of Oven Mouth and Howe Edge.

The route leads down the pleasant pastures into wild Whitsundale with plenty of pretty waterfalls. You will reach the two-house hamlet of Ravenseat, a former drover trading post which once boasted 11 households, a pub and a chapel. At the first house, turn left along the track and cross the ancient packhorse bridge over the Whitsundale Beck. Walk up the road where the Coast to Coast Walk leaves for Nine Standards Rigg, and past the house called Black How with a signpost "Footpath to Hoggarth Bridge." Ignore this and yards up the road, turn left by the moor wall, unless you want to follow the unfenced moor road with very little traffic down to the B6270.

Back on the main route, the map should be consulted frequently. Hug the wall, cross a ladder stile, keep by the wall and pass a couple of barns on your left to cross a stile in the same stone wall. Go down a rough undulating pasture, boggy and pathless, and aim between the open gap in the ruined corner wall. Note the superb views of the gorge at Oven Mouth and Howe Edge, already seen on the outward route. Go up the tufty pasture, cross a stile in the facing hidden wall on your left, pass another barn and through a gated stile, the only one waymarked on this downhill route. Cross a final field to come out on to the B6270.

Turn left along the road, cross High Bridge over the River Swale and follow the road (busy in summer) for an easy finish, of one and a half miles back to Keld. It is a long road walk compensated with fine views of Wain Wath Force, Rainby Force and Currack Force.

© Crown Copyright

GILLING WEST
An attractive village - Best Kept Village 1987 (START & FINISH)

To A66 Melsonby 2 miles
To Skeeby 2 miles
Gilling Beck
B6274
To Richmond 3 miles

To Barnard Castle - 12 miles

Gilling Bridge

Water Lane (Broad bridleway)

Mill Farm

Acre Farm

Hartforth Beck

HARTFORTH
A tiny hamlet

Easy field paths via stiles/kissing gates

Hartforth Hall

Footbridge

Hartforth Saw Mill (Follow yellow arrows)

Crabtree House

Scant remains of old lead mill

Six stepping stones

JAGGER LANE
An ancient packhorse route

Gill Beck

Leadmill

Plank Bridge

Hartforth Wood

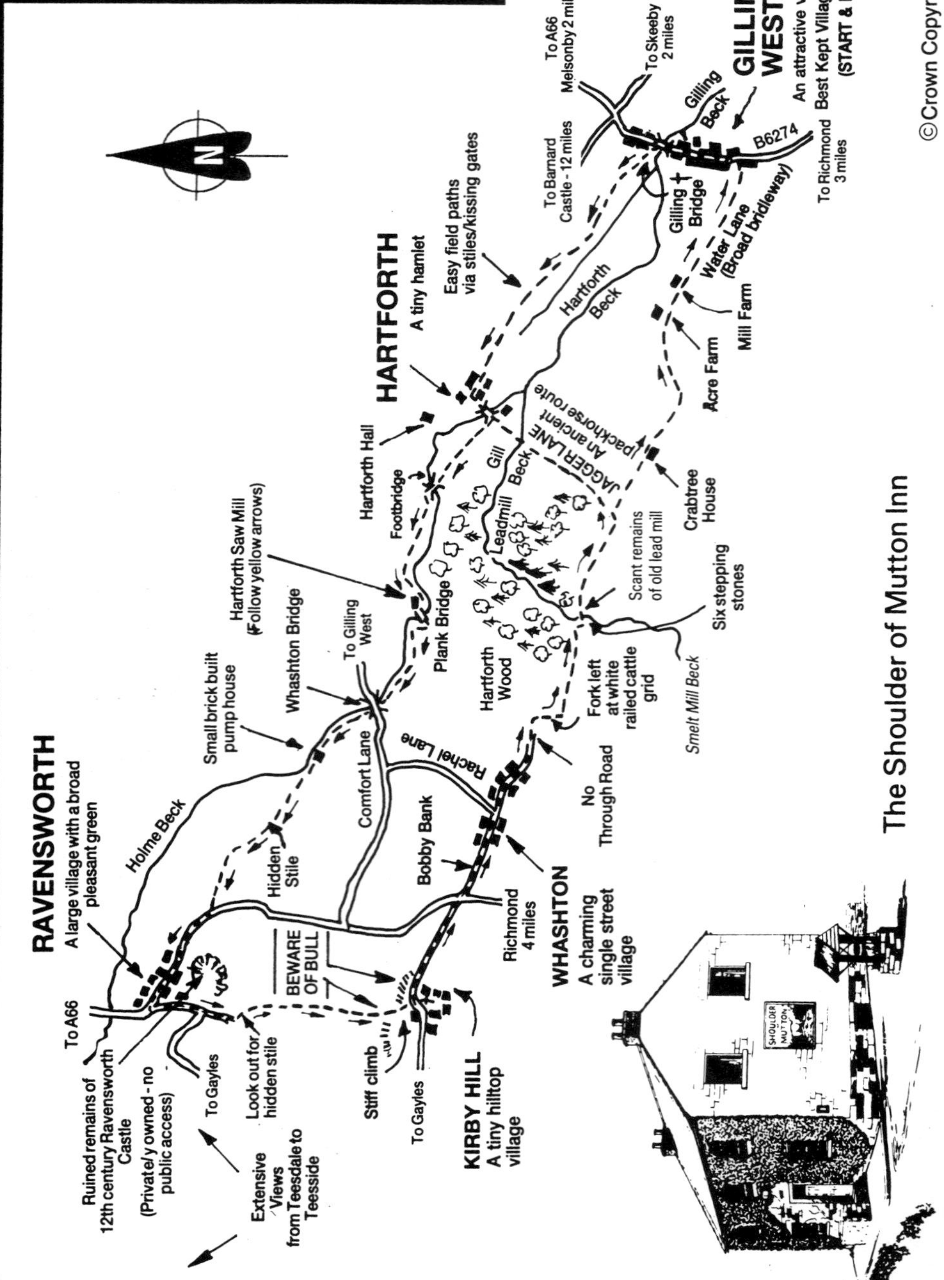

Smelt Mill Beck

Fork left at white railed cattle grid

Whashton Bridge

To Gilling West

Small brick built pump house

RAVENSWORTH
A large village with a broad pleasant green

Holme Beck

Ruined remains of 12th century Ravensworth Castle
(Privately owned - no public access)

To A66

To Gayles

Extensive Views from Teesdale to Teesside

Look out for hidden stile

BEWARE OF BULL

Hidden Stile

Comfort Lane

Rachel Lane

Bobby Bank

No Through Road

WHASHTON
A charming single street village

Richmond 4 miles

Stiff climb

To Gayles

KIRBY HILL
A tiny hilltop village

The Shoulder of Mutton Inn

13. Gilling West

Route: *Gilling West — Hartforth — Ravensworth — Kirby Hill — Whashton — Gilling West.*

Distance: *About 8 miles (13 km). Allow 4½/5 hours. Fairly easy to moderate. All field path walk with one stiff climb. Some road walking.*

O.S. Maps: *Landranger Sheet 92; Pathfinder 1:25,000 Sheet NZ10.*

Parking: *Limited parking outside St Agatha's Church, High Street, Gilling West.*

Public Transport: *United Services 29, Darlington to Richmond; Barnard Castle Coaches Service 79, Barnard Castle to Richmond.*

Refreshments: *The Angel Inn, The White Swan Inn, Gilling West; The Bay Horse, Ravensworth; Shoulder of Mutton Inn, Kirby Hill; The Hack and Spade, Whashton.*

Take a walk in the valley without a name and enjoy the charming countryside between the picturesque villages of Gilling West, Ravensworth, Kirby Hill and Whashton, all situated south of the busy A66. This rewarding ramble is one of the best in Richmondshire and recommended for any time of the year.

Start this walk from the pleasant village of Gilling West and at the north end of Gilling Bridge, turn left at the public footpath signpost and go through the wall gap with the handgate missing. Pass Town End Farm (dated 1906) and walk westwards for an easy walk, mainly through the middle of most of the fields for a mile, to the hidden hamlet of Hartforth.

Although it is a direct and well-defined route through stiles and handgates, after 440 yards in the field with a scarecrow, pass to the right of this and veer left below some stone barn buildings for a hidden stile. In Hartforth, you join the Jagger Lane, one of the oldest highways in Richmondshire. This pack pony trail, used by and named after ponies called Jagger, was an important salt, lead and coal road between Durham and Wensleydale.

Turn left by the barn buildings, follow the broad track and cross the ornate bridge over the Hartforth Beck. Here you leave the Jagger Lane. Turn right through the white gate and follow the path between the growing crops, noting the views of Hartforth Hall with its ruined church remains.

Cross the metal footbridge over the beck and turn left round the field edge by the beck for a rough walk — it is tough on the feet. Exit through a gap by a rusty gate and turn left along a track to the century-old Hartforth Saw Mill, which ceased operations about 20 years ago. Here, yellow way-mark arrows direct you left round by the mill to cross a plank bridge and a stile by a gate.

Turn right upstream for a lovely walk through lush meadows, stiled and gated to come into the quaintly-named Comfort Lane at Whashton Bridge. South of the bridge, on the opposite side of the lane, cross the stile and upstream follow the Holme Beck and look out for the herons.

After you pass a small brick-built pump house and where the beck bends right (check map), walk straight on, in single file over the centre of the cultivated field with no sign of a path and aim for a stile, where the hedge ends. Cross not one, but two stiles and aim for the top inset right corner of the lush meadow. Cross the concealed stile by a gate in the hawthorn bushes on your right and forward, look for another stile beyond the holly and hawthorn bushes. Turn left through the stone stile and diagonally right over the next two stiled pastures, with excellent views of the twelfth century ruined remains of Ravensworth Castle, once the stronghold of the Fitzhugh family.

At the road, turn right for 880 yards into the delightful village of Ravensworth, with fine houses grouped around a lovely large green. Before you reach the Bay Horse, which serves bar meals, turn left down the road, pass the primary school for another view of the impressive sight of the ruined castle (privately-owned with no public access).

Where the lane bends right, go through the handgate by the gate marked "Larklands" and proceed up the track for a short way. Straddle a stream and go through the hidden stile between two ash trees on your left. Diagonally ascend the rough pasture and aim for the stile, where the wall ends and the hawthorn hedge starts and vice versa. Go up the edge of two fields with oil seed rape crops. In the next field prepare for a stiff climb up the hillside and if the grazing bull is still around, you will reach the hilltop village of Kirby Hill in quick time.

Explore this tiny village dominated by the church built in 1397 and dedicated to St Peter and St Felix. Here there is an excellent opportunity for buying refreshments at the ivy-clad country inn called the Shoulder of Mutton. Walkers are certainly welcome.

Walk back out of the village and take the road by the church, noting the fine panorama from Teesdale to Teesside. In 440 yards, cross straight over the crossroads and walk up Bobby's Bank for another 440 yards into the elevated single street village of Whashton, with neat cottages and neat gardens. At the bottom of the village, bear right and follow the No Through Road, a quiet country lane downhill for about 440 yards and when you cross the white-railed cattle grid, turn immediately left along the field to exit through a gate.

(Continued on page 50)

49

(Continued from page 49)

Follow the path uphill between the trees by Hartforth Wood and go down the well-worn path to cross six stepping stones over Leadmill Gill Beck. As you climb out of this wooded valley, note the ruined remains of the old lead smelt mill.

At the top, follow Smelt Mill Beck eastwards for another brief encounter of the Jagger Lane. Turn left along this old highway for only a few yards, leave it and turn right eastwards along a broad farm road for a steady climb up past Crabtree House Farm and down into Waters Lane. Follow this farm road for an easy return back to Gilling West.

Fore Gill Gate from Reeth Low Moor (Walk 7, p35).

Low Linn Falls near Eastgate (Walk 27, p106).

At Kidhow Gate looking back to Hawes (Walk 17, p64).

The arched bridge in Beck Hole village (Walk 2, p8).

14. Keld

Route: *Keld — Tan Hill — Ravenseat — Keld.*
Distance: *Over 10 miles (16km). Strenuous. Tough trek over wild and featureless moors. Allow 6/7 hours.*
O.S.Maps: *Landranger Sheets 91 or 92; Outdoor Leisure Map 30. Compass necessary.*
Parking: *Limited roadside parking in Keld. Do not obstruct gateways. Farm access, please keep clear.*
Public Transport: *United Services No 30, Richmond — Keld. Check timetables.*
Refreshments: *Tan Hill Inn, bar snacks and meals.*
Warning: *Do not stray from the Pennine Way and keep away from the coal pit shafts near Tan Hill. In uncertain weather, there are escape routes. Use the road from Tan Hill down West Stonesdale to Keld. Soggy moorland paths with peat bogs, stout footwear necessary. You can easily come astray on this walk, so don't forget the relevant Ordnance Survey Map; Outdoor Leisure Map recommended. A fine clear day with good visibility is essential, do not attempt in doubtful weather.*

Using part of the Pennine Way, and the Coast to Coast Walk, this walk goes in search of the lost highway between Tan Hill and Ravenseat.

Called the Jagger Road or Coal Road, it was used by packhorse traffic carrying coal from Tan Hill pit to Kirkby Stephen, during the seventeenth century.

This upland walk is quite strenuous, and in places often wet and boggy. It explores the wilderness of West Stonesdale, giving splendid views of shadowy summits, and takes you to the Tan Hill Inn, the highest hostelry in the country.

At the bottom of Keld Village, leave by the sign "Public Footpath to Muker", and follow Keld Lane for 400 yards to a double Pennine Way sign which directs you left down to the River Swale. Cross the footbridge and walk up by East Gill Force, the first of half-a-dozen waterfalls seen on this walk.

Above the waterfall, the Pennine Way coincides with the Coast to Coast Walk. Turn left along the farm track and climb up to East Stonesdale Farm, where the Coast to Coast Walk heads westwards for Ravenseat — part of the return route of this walk. The Pennine Way heads northwards up the enclosed lane, and out on to Black Moor and along the 1,400 foot moor ridge through gated fell pastures with backward views of Great Shunner Fell and Lovely Seat.

Below Low Firth Farm, journey northwards over the sodden Stonesdale Moor and sample some bog-hopping. Onwards, cross Lad Gill and turn right up Lad Gill Hill with westwards views to Nine Standards Rigg (nine tall cairns of unknown origin).

Follow the peaty path which becomes a level grass track, passing a fenced pit shaft (danger) to reach Tan Hill Inn, advertised as Great Britain's highest inn at 1,732 feet above sea level and situated a few yards into County Durham. This lonely pub of double-glazing advertising fame was the focal point for drovers, miners and pedlars traversing the drovers roads between Yorkshire, Durham and Westmorland. Today, it is a mecca for Pennine Way walkers and tourists.

From the pub, take the Keld road for 250 yards to reach a footpath signpost on your right marked "Ravenseat 3 miles". Here you must decide whether to return to Keld by road, or follow the old Jagger Road. Turn right, south-west down the faint fellside path by Tan Gill to trace the lost Jagger Road. It is hard to imagine that this was once a busy highway with packhorse traffic!

At the bottom, stride Tan Gill and follow the Stonesdale Beck until you see a second sheepfold, then cross the plank bridge over the beck and pass the sheep pens.

Climb up the south side of Thomas Gill, and at the top, do not cross the gill although the right of way is shown on the O.S. map along the north side of it. Turn left (south) along a path on Thomas Gill Rigg (1,700ft) with superb views all around.

When the path peters out (the Jagger Road is lost) aim for the wire boundary fence seen above, and follow this along to your left until it turns left, then straddle the corner fence with large stones on either side. On the ground you will see the words — Ordnance Survey Trigonometrical Station.

Turn left, hug the fence, avoid the peat bogs and as the fence dips, bear south-west, half right to the roofless ruins of Robert's Seat House, a watch house built for watchers or gamekeepers who protected the moors from poachers in the fourteenth century.

From this spot, aim for the TV mast and head south over a way-marked stile to follow the way-marked posts into the valley. Ford Hoods Bottom Beck, pass Jenny Whalley Force (I wonder who she was?) to reach the two-house hamlet of Ravenseat with its interesting packhorse bridge. This hamlet was once a drovers trading post.

You leave the Jagger Road and join the Coast to Coast Walk for the three mile return route from Ravenseat to Keld. Follow the yellow way-marks and signposts with detailed direction not necessary, first along by the beck with cascading water-

(Continued on page 57)

55

14. Keld

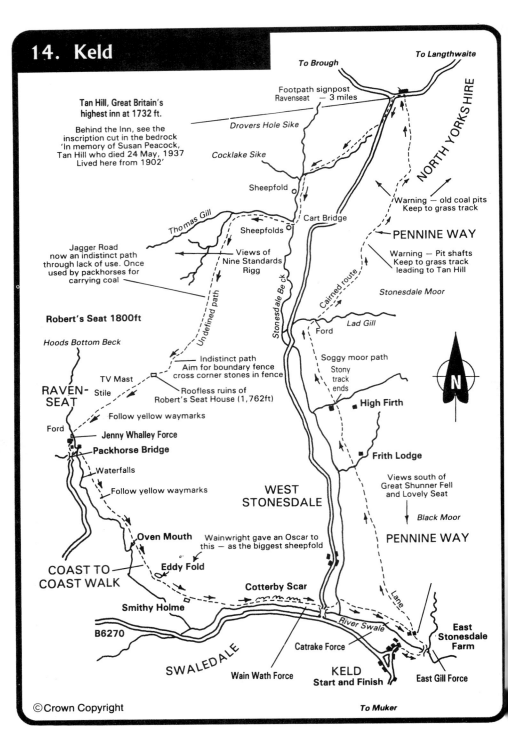

Tan Hill, Great Britain's highest inn at 1732 ft.

Behind the Inn, see the inscription cut in the bedrock 'In memory of Susan Peacock, Tan Hill who died 24 May, 1937 Lived here from 1902'

To Brough

To Langthwaite

Footpath signpost Ravenseat — 3 miles

NORTH YORKSHIRE

Drovers Hole Sike

Cocklake Sike

Warning — old coal pits Keep to grass track

PENNINE WAY

Sheepfold

Thomas Gill

Cart Bridge

Sheepfolds

Warning — Pit shafts Keep to grass track leading to Tan Hill

Views of Nine Standards Rigg

Jagger Road now an indistinct path through lack of use. Once used by packhorses for carrying coal

Stonesdale Beck

Cairned route

Stonesdale Moor

Robert's Seat 1800ft

Hoods Bottom Beck

Ford

Lad Gill

Undefined path

Indistinct path Aim for boundary fence cross corner stones in fence

Soggy moor path Stony track ends

TV Mast

RAVEN-SEAT   Stile

Roofless ruins of Robert's Seat House (1,762ft)

High Firth

Follow yellow waymarks

Ford

Jenny Whalley Force

Packhorse Bridge

Frith Lodge

Waterfalls

Follow yellow waymarks

WEST STONESDALE

Views south of Great Shunner Fell and Lovely Seat

Black Moor

PENNINE WAY

Oven Mouth

Wainwright gave an Oscar to this — as the biggest sheepfold

COAST TO COAST WALK

Eddy Fold

Cotterby Scar

Lane

Smithy Holme

River Swale

East Stonesdale Farm

B6270

SWALEDALE

Catrake Force

KELD Start and Finish

East Gill Force

Wain Wath Force

© Crown Copyright

To Muker

(Continued from page 55)

falls, then up along the gated pastures above the dramatic gorge of Howe Edge and Oven Mouth.

Further on, take the lower path, pass below Eddy Fold, awarded an Oscar by Alfred Wainwright for being the biggest sheepfold ever seen! Again, take the lower path, pass behind Smithy Holme (empty farmhouse) and below another farm, turn left through the open gap in the the wall and traverse eastwards above the long escarpment of Cotterby Scar with Wain Wath Force below.

At the hairpin bend of the road, turn left up this and take the farm road to East Stonesdale Farm, passing Currack Force and return by the outward route to Keld.

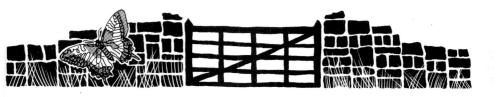

15. Castle Bolton

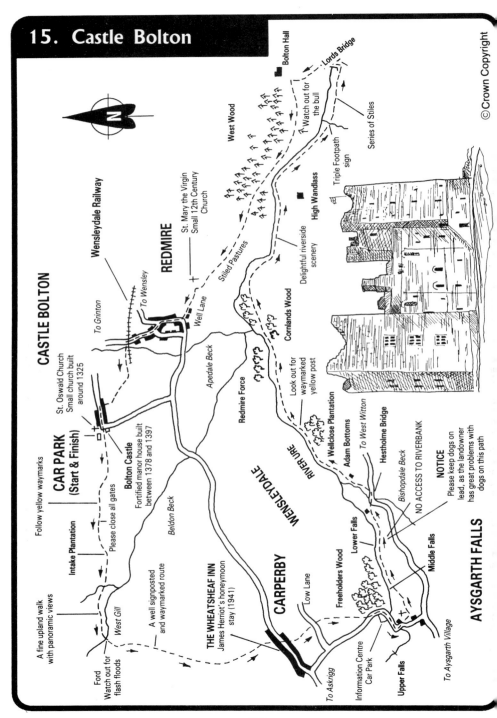

CASTLE BOLTON

Follow yellow waymarks

CAR PARK (Start & Finish)

St. Oswald Church
Small church built around 1325

Wensleydale Railway

To Grinton

To Wensley

REDMIRE

St. Mary the Virgin
Small 12th Century Church

Well Lane

Intake Plantation

Please close all gates

Bolton Castle
Fortified manor house built between 1378 and 1397

Apedale Beck

West Wood

Bolton Hall

Lords Bridge

Watch out for the bull

Series of Stiles

Triple Footpath sign

High Wandlass

Delightful riverside scenery

Stilted Pastures

Cornlands Wood

Look out for waymarked yellow post

Redmire Force

WENSLEYDALE

Wellclose Plantation

Beldon Beck

A fine upland walk with panoramic views

Ford
Watch out for flash floods

West Gill

A well signposted and waymarked route

THE WHEATSHEAF INN
James Herriot's honeymoon stay (1941)

CARPERBY

Low Lane

To Askrigg

RIVER URE

Adam Bottoms

To West Witton

Hestholme Bridge

Bishopdale Beck

NOTICE
Please keep dogs on lead, as the landowner has great problems with dogs on this path

NO ACCESS TO RIVERBANK

Freeholders Wood

Lower Falls

Middle Falls

Upper Falls

Information Centre Car Park

To Aysgarth Village

AYSGARTH FALLS

15. Castle Bolton

Route: Castle Bolton — Carperby — Aysgarth Falls — Redmire Force — Lords Bridge — Redmire — Castle Bolton.

Distance: Over 11 miles (18km). Moderate. Allow 6/7 hours. A high and low level walk with panoramic views.

O.S. Maps: Landranger Sheet 98. Outdoor Leisure 30.

Parking: Castle Bolton car park. Honesty box — fee 40p.

Refreshments: Tearoom, Bolton Castle; The Wheatsheaf Inn, Carperby; Dales Park Cafe, Aysgarth National Park Centre; Mill Race Tea Shop, The Falls Motel and The Palmer Flatts Hotel, Aysgarth Falls; The Bolton Arms and The Kings Arms, Redmire.

Note: Bolton Castle — open every day March-November inclusive; 10am — 5pm (adults £1.50, children & OAPs 75p.

This walk is a concise description, so carry the relevant Ordnance Survey maps which are needed on the route to Redmire Force between Hestholme Bridge and Lords Bridge. Although way-marked, stiled and signposted, it is less well-known and you will encounter some pathless fields, so constantly check the map. Please keep dogs under control at all times.

Some of the finest scenery in Wensleydale rewards this walk, which visits Bolton Castle and the famous Aysgarth Falls, as well as Redmire Force, one of the least-known waterfalls on the River Ure.

This high and low level loop is a classic, with superb views and delightful riverside scenery.

If you have time, visit Bolton Castle, the historic fortress where Mary Queen of Scots was imprisoned. Opposite the castle, the tiny St. Oswald's Church warrants a visit.

The three-mile outward route from Castle Bolton to Aysgarth Falls is clearly signposted and way-marked. This fine upland route, with gentle gradients, offers panoramic views over Wensleydale to Penhill, Walden and Bishopdale.

From Castle Bolton car park, turn right, cross the stile signposted "Aysgarth 3 miles" and walk westwards along the unsurfaced, gated track through the fields of Bolton Parks. On the way, close all gates and do not be surprised to see a bull among the grazing cattle.

After 1½ miles, ford West Gill (subject to flash floods) and beyond, go through a gate signposted Carperby' and follow the path over a long rough pasture dotted with hawthorn trees. Continue through another signposted gate, head downhill, where a triple signpost directs you left for 880 yards into Carperby.

Turn right along the village to the Wheatsheaf Inn (James Herriot's honeymoon stay, 1941), here opposite, go through a gate and then left, southwards to Low Lane. Opposite, cross the stile and follow the path through the stiled fields into Freeholders Wood, where you bear right downhill to the Carperby road.

Turn left down the road (no footway for 300 yards), pass under the railway bridge to reach Aysgarth Falls National Park Centre, where you can easily explore the famous three waterfalls, Upper, Middle and Lower Falls.

St Oswald's Church, Castle Bolton

Cross Yore Bridge, view the Upper Falls and visit the Craft Centre and the Yorkshire Carriage Museum, both housed in Yore Mill. By the museum, climb the steps up to St. Andrew's Church which is well worth a visit. Pass in front of the church and through the churchyard, cross a stile and over the field, cross another stile and walk within the woodland edge, where a notice, strongly urges you to keep dogs on a lead.

Keep by the field edge, above the wooded riverside giving glimpses of the Middle Falls and further on, the Lower Falls. Remember there is no access to the riverbank. Follow this popular path which brings you out at the entrance to Hestholme Farm on the busy A684 road.

Turn left along the main road, cross Hestholme Bridge over Bishopdale Beck and take the first stile on your left, marked 'Wensley 4½'. Follow the path eastwards by the River Ure and enjoy the delightful riverside scenery. En route, pass a way-marked barn, cross a stile and through a gate to follow the right of way behind the stone built farm called Adam Bottoms. Beyond the farm, follow the way-

(Continued on page 60)

(Continued from page 59)

marks through four stiled/gated fields by the riverside.

Leave the riverside and climb the steep woodland path up Wellclose Plantation, where at the top, cross a signposted stile. Turn left and watch out for a yellow marker post, which directs you to the top of the same field and turn right along the elevated stiled, path giving good views northwards to Bolton Castle. Eastwards over four more fields (1½ miles from Hestholme), cross a high ladder stile into Cornlands Wood and descend the stepped path to Redmire Force, a delightful series of small waterfalls.

Follow the footpath signs out of the wood and left along a field of drumlins and over another high ladder stile. Continue eastwards over pastures, sometimes pathless, until you see High Wanless (farm) away to your right, where you rejoin the gated riverside path to reach a stream. Here a triple signpost points the way, eastwards through a series of stiled fields to a tree-lined lane.

Turn left along the lane, cross the arched Lords Bridge over the River Ure and follow the driveway through the lovely parkland of Bolton Hall. Look out for the grazing bull! As you approach the hall, go through a gate, turn left and follow the track to West Wood for a mile and exit through a tall kissing gate. Follow a series of stiled pastures for another mile via Well Lane to reach Redmire.

Turn right up the village and opposite Hogra Farm, bear left by the village hall and pass the Bolton Arms. Beyond the school, go under the railway bridge and turn left at the footpath sign and follow the path parallel to the Wensleydale Railway which serves the Redmire Quarry.

The mile route to Castle Bolton crosses a couple of footbridges and passes the railway end, where in 1964, the Northallerton-Hawes line closed. Proceed up the stiled pastures to the lovely village of Castle Bolton for a splendid finish.

16. Aysgarth Falls

Route: *Aysgarth Falls — Eshington Bridge — West Burton — Morpeth Gate — Templars' Chapel — Hudson Quarry Lane — Blue Bridge — Eshington Bridge — Hestholme Bridge — Aysgarth Falls.*
Distance: *About 8½ miles (13.5km). Allow 4½ hours. Fairly easy to moderate.*
Parking: *Aysgarth Falls car park. Pay and display.*
O.S. Maps: *Landranger Sheet 98; Outdoor Leisure Sheet 30.*
Public Transport: *United Services: Richmond to Hawes (check timetables).*
Refreshments: *The Mill Race Tea Shop. The Palmer Flatts Hotel, Aysgarth Falls; The Fox and Hounds, West Burton.*
Note: *Observe the notices — "Please keep dogs on a lead" and "No Access to Riverbank". This is a concise description so carry the relevant O.S. maps. Plenty of mud, stout footwear advisable.*

This attractive walk around Aysgarth is without doubt, one of the finest in mid Wensleydale. Certainly, it is a favourite for waterfalls, popular paths and panoramic views.

Although one long walk is described, two shorter walks are available by using the paths shown on the map. Both can commence either at Aysgarth Falls or West Burton.

From Aysgarth Falls car park, take the paved path to Yore Bridge with excellent views of the Upper Falls. By Yore Mill and the Carriage Museum, climb the steps to St. Andrew's Church and southwards up the churchyard into Church Lane to reach the A684. Cross the road and almost opposite, go through the gated stile, signposted "Eshington Bridge" with a request "Meadowland — Single file, Please". Walk straight on and at the end of the field, admire the views over to Penhill, West Burton, Waldendale and Bishopdale.

Cross the stile, go down and up the hidden dry valley of Thieves Gill. Cross a stile and another (check map) then turn southwards down the stiled fields to reach Eshington Bridge, noting the stile on the left of the bridge, which is the beckside return route for both the long and short walks back to Aysgarth Falls.

Cross the bridge over the Bishopdale Beck, and turn right through a signposted stile with another request to keep in single file. Walk straight on, cross another way-marked stile and keep by the wall to reach a corner way-marked post, then bear half left over the field to cross a corner stile near the beck.

Now head southwards over the next two way-marked fields to cross the busy B6160. Climb the steps and follow the narrow walled path to come out opposite 'Meadowcroft' in West Burton. There is plenty of time to explore this pretty village on the way back from the next part of the walk.

Immediately turn left down Back Nook which joins Front Nook and pass The Grange, an impressive Georgian Mansion to join the B6160. Opposite Grange Farm Cottage, cross Burton Bridge, an ancient packhorse bridge over the Walden Beck. It is signposted "Unsuitable for Motors".

Now follow the walled lane, an ancient highway

St Andrew's Church, Aysgarth

that once linked Middleham with Bainbridge, for 1½ miles passing Flanders Hall (dated 1779) and Howraine, both on your left. As you gradually climb up Morpeth Gate meaning "murder path", see the superb views westwards to West Burton, and up Bishopdale. When the lane swings right uphill, go through the green metal on your left, signposted "F.P. Templars Chapel 1 mile".

Follow the path and near the end of this first field, a double footpath sign directs you uphill through a wooden gate. Turn left and walk eastwards along the next five stiled/way-marked fields with detailed directions not necessary. You will reach the ruined remains of Penhill Preceptory, an ancient chapel of the Knights Templar, which was built c1200 and uncovered in 1840. Explore the chapel ruins with three foot walls and tiny stone coffins.

From the chapel, bear half right, diagonally up the same field for the metal gate wedged between the woods. Once through the gate, note the boundary stone on your right marked with a cross symbol and dated 1865. When you reach the concrete track, turn right up this and follow it for ½ mile to High Lane. There are some superb views of Wensleydale dominated by Penhill.

(Continued on page 63)

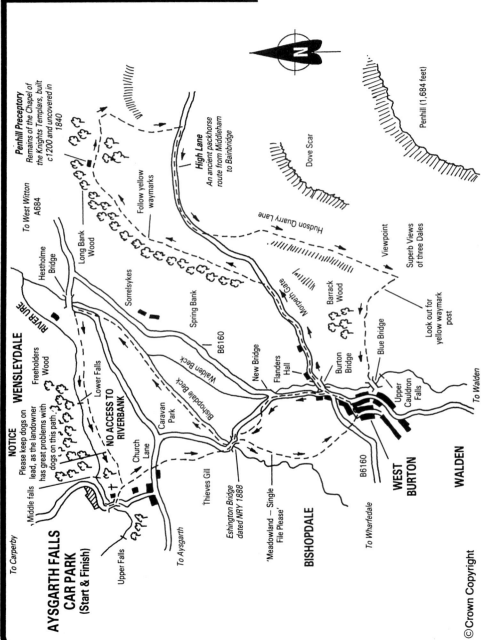

AYSGARTH FALLS CAR PARK (Start & Finish)

To Carperby

Upper Falls

Middle falls

NOTICE
Please keep dogs on lead, as the landowner has great problems with dogs on this path

Freeholders Wood

WENSLEYDALE

NO ACCESS TO RIVERBANK

Lower Falls

Church Lane

To Aysgarth

Thieves Gill

RIVER URE

Hestholme Bridge

To West Witton A684

Long Bank Wood

Sorrelsykes

Caravan Park

Eshington Bridge dated NRY 1888

'Meadowland — Single File Please'

BISHOPDALE

To Wharfedale

Bishopdale Beck

Walden Beck

B6160

Spring Bank

New Bridge

Flanders Hall

Penhill Preceptory
Remains of the Chapel of the Knights Templars, built c1200 and uncovered in 1840

High Lane
An ancient packhorse route from Middleham to Bainbridge

Follow yellow waymarks

Morpeth Gate

Hudson Quarry Lane

Dove Scar

Penhill (1,684 feet)

Viewpoint
Superb Views of three Dales

Barrack Wood

Look out for yellow waymark post

Blue Bridge

Burton Bridge

Upper Cauldron Falls

B6160

WEST BURTON

WALDEN

To Walden

©Crown Copyright

(Continued from page 61)

Turn right along this broad walled lane, used during cattle droving days, for ½ mile.

Where the lane divides below Dove Scar and above Morpeth Scar, you can shorten the walk by going straight down the lane via Morpeth Gate to West Burton, but if you fancy an airy upland walk, then turn left up the signposted path "West Burton via Hudson Quarry Lane 1½ miles".

Follow this elevated lane and experience some glorious fell walking with superb views of three dales — Waldendale, Bishopdale and Wensleydale dominated by Buckden Pike (2,302ft). At the lane end, turn right in front of the gate, signposted "West Burton", descend the terrace fellslope and aim for a way-marked post on the fell edge, with roof top views of West Burton below.

From here, descend steeply, the zig zag path between the tree stumps guided by way-marked posts. At the bottom, cross a stile, turn left and enter the edge of Barrack Wood and out into pleasant pastures. Head south down the next couple of fields, way-marked/stiled and down some steps to cross Blue Bridge (dated 1860) over Walden Beck. Here admire the Upper Cauldron Falls, a delightful secluded waterfall.

Turn right between Waterfall Cottage and The Mill to re-enter West Burton, one of Wensleydale's loveliest villages and certainly most photographed place in Yorkshire. It has a spacious green with a spire cross and stocks. The Fox and Hounds offers refreshments.

At the bottom of the village, turn left along Front Nook, noting the Lower Cauldron Falls, pass The Grange again and follow the Aysgarth Road. Where the footway ends, go through the stile on your left and turn right along the field for 250 yards with the wall on your right. This path avoids further road walking.

Turn right over a stile and back out on to the same road. Turn left over Eshington Bridge and cross the stile on your right, already mentioned on the outward route. It is signposted "Hestholme".

Follow the stiled path eastwards by the Bishopdale Beck which takes you through Westholme Caravan Park. On the way, the Walden Beck joins the Bishopdale Beck. When you reach the busy A684, turn right for 250 yards and at the entrance to Hestholme, cross the signposted stile on your left. Cross the field diagonally to another stile and join the riverside route.

On the last leg of this walk, you are strongly urged to keep dogs on a lead and notices advise you that there is no access to the riverbank. If you keep to the path and follow the signposted/stiled pastures, you should have no problems with this riverside route. Look out for the Lower Falls, as well as the Middle Falls on the way back. Emerge into the churchyard, pass St. Andrew's Church and return by the outward route to Aysgarth Falls car park.

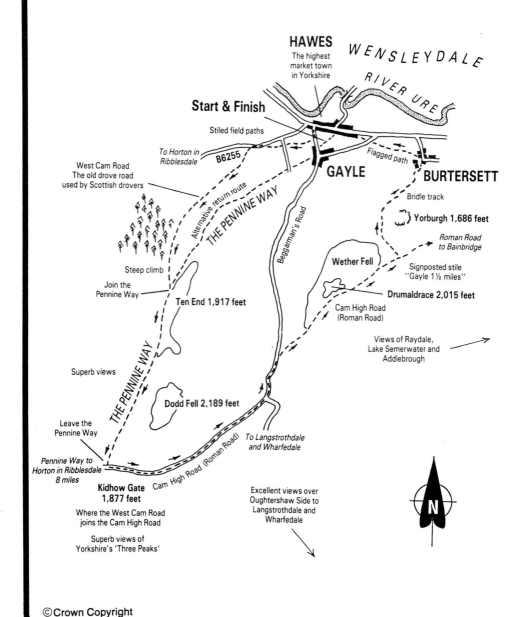

HAWES
The highest market town in Yorkshire

WENSLEYDALE

RIVER URE

Start & Finish

Stiled field paths

To Horton in Ribblesdale

B6255

West Cam Road
The old drove road used by Scottish drovers

Flagged path

GAYLE

BURTERSETT

Bridle track

Alternative return route

THE PENNINE WAY

Beggarman's Road

Yorburgh 1,686 feet

Roman Road to Bainbridge

Steep climb

Join the Pennine Way

Wether Fell

Signposted stile "Gayle 1½ miles"

Drumaldrace 2,015 feet

Ten End 1,917 feet

Cam High Road (Roman Road)

Views of Raydale, Lake Semerwater and Addlebrough

Superb views

THE PENNINE WAY

Dodd Fell 2,189 feet

Leave the Pennine Way

To Langstrothdale and Wharfedale

Pennine Way to Horton in Ribblesdale 8 miles

Cam High Road (Roman Road)

Kidhow Gate 1,877 feet

Where the West Cam Road joins the Cam High Road

Superb views of Yorkshire's 'Three Peaks'

Excellent views over Oughtershaw Side to Langstrothdale and Wharfedale

N

17. Hawes

Route: *Hawes — West Cam Road — Ten End — Kidhow Gate — Cam Road — Wether Fell — Burtersett — Hawes.*
Distance: *Under 13 miles (20km). Allow 6½ to 7 hours. Strenuous with a demanding steep climb. Some road walking.*
O.S. Maps: *Landranger Sheet 98; Outdoor Leisure Sheets 30 and 31.*
Parking: *Car park in Gayle Lane, at the west end of Hawes.*
Public Transport: *United services — Richmond to Hawes (check timetable)*
Refreshments: *Plenty of pubs and cafes in Hawes.*
Note: *Map and compass essential. A fine clear day with good visibility is needed. Always be prepared for the worst. Expect plenty of mud.*

This airy upland walk follows in the footsteps of the drovers along the ancient highways around Hawes in Upper Wensleydale. It is a great high level walk giving marvellous views of a dozen or more of Yorkshire's highest fells.

The walk starts from the car park in Gayle Lane, at the west end of Hawes. Go up the lane and, opposite the Wensleydale Creameries, cross the stile signposted "Mossy Lane" and follow the path westwards through five stiled fields to Mossy Lane, noting the views northwards of Great Shunner Fell (2,340ft), Lovely Seat (2,213 ft), Stags Fell, Hugh Seat (2,257 ft) and High Seat (2,328 ft), while backward views reveal Addlebrough (1,864 ft) and Wether Fell (2,105 ft).

Continue through the next couple of stiled fields (watch out — duck under the high wire above the last stile), to reach the busy B6255. Turn left up the road for 150 yards and where it bends right, go up the walled lane which is the old drovers road called the West Cam Road. Ascend this stony enclosed track for a stiff climb and at the top, cross a ladder stile, right of a gate. Pause here and look at the unfolding views of the surrounding summits. See if you can spot Hawes and Hardraw, Cotterdale, Wild Boar Fell and Baugh Fell, Widdale Fell with Great Knoutberry Hill and Whernside (2,419 ft), Yorkshire's highest summit.

Stride out, south-westwards along the open fell track over Backsides with fine views into the Snaizeholme valley below. Pass the Snaizeholme forest plantation on your right and follow the stony track uphill for a stiff steep climb, with good views of Ingleborough (2,373 ft), Yorkshire's magic mountain. Pity the poor pack ponies that had to climb this steep stony gradient.

Two miles from the B6255, there is a cairn on your left with white-painted words "Cam Road/ P.W.Hawes". You have now reached the Pennine Way on the western flanks of Ten End (1,917 ft). To shorten the walk, turn left and follow the Pennine Way down the cairned flanks of Ten End to Gayle and back to Hawes.

For the main route, turn right along the high level green lane for a windswept walk, giving marvellous views of mountain and moor. Follow this packhorse route for a further 2½ miles along the flanks of DoddFell (2,189 ft), to reach the double Pennine Way signpost (Horton 8 miles/Hawes 5 miles) at Kidhow Gate (GR 830834), which is the junction of the West Cam Road and the Cam High Road.

This is one of the finest viewpoints in the Yorkshire Dales. What a grand view of Yorkshire's Three Peaks plus Fountains Fell and many more shadowy summits. Here you part company with the Pennine Way, and turn left along the open-gated Cam High Road (Roman road) for 2½ miles, giving good views over Oughtershaw Side into Wharfedale with Buckden Pike prominent.

At the Hawes-Kettlewell road, continue straight on for 880 yards and just before the Beggarmans Road descends, turn right along the walled Cam Road and follow this Roman road route for a couple of miles, by the flanks of Drumaldrace and Wether Fell. Here you will see Stalling Busk and Lake Semerwater, Pen Hill and Addlebrough.

At the footpath signpost "Gayle 1½ miles", cross the wall stile on your left and walk straight on over the brow of the fell, where the path veers right and curves left, then leads you downhill to a facing stone wall, with no stile. Straddle the wall and follow the well-worn path through an open gateway with a nearby corrugated hut.

A word of warning — this is the wettest part of the walk. Follow the winding bridle track downhill for two more miles to the village of Burtersett, noting the wonderful views of Upper Wensleydale. In this tiny village, turn right in front of Meadow Cottage and as you turn left down the street, on your right is Hillary Hall, built in 1729 and named after the Hillary family, whose descendant, Sir Edmund Hillary conquered Mount Everest.

Just beyond the Methodist Church (erected 1870, enlarged 1904) turn left alongside the church and follow the path through a gated stile, and out into the open fields. For the return to Hawes, the route is paved throughout with sandstone flagstones which are easy to follow as you head westwards over the stiled pastures via Old Gayle Lane for a final field walk of ¾ mile to come out just beyond Wensleydale Press on the A684. Turn left along the main road to end the walk back in Hawes.

18. Semerwater

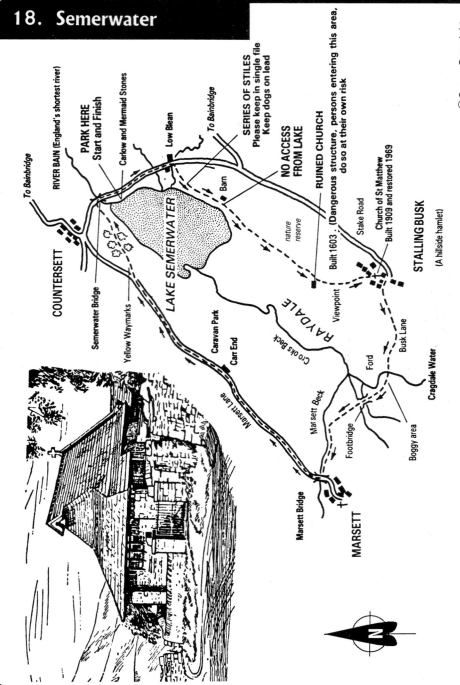

© Crown Copyright

To Bainbridge

COUNTERSETT

RIVER BAIN (England's shortest river!)

PARK HERE
Start and Finish

Carlow and Mermaid Stones

Low Bean

To Bainbridge

SERIES OF STILES
Please keep in single file
Keep dogs on lead

NO ACCESS
FROM LAKE

Barn

RUINED CHURCH
Built 1603 . (Dangerous
structure, persons entering this area,
do so at their own risk

Stake Road

Church of St Matthew
Built 1909 and restored 1969

STALLING BUSK
(A hillside hamlet)

LAKE SEMERWATER

nature
reserve

Viewpoint

Semerwater Bridge

Yellow Waymarks

Caravan Park

Carr End

Crooks Beck

RAYDALE

Ford

Busk Lane

Cragdale Water

Marsett Lane

Marsett Beck

Footbridge

Boggy area

Marsett Bridge

MARSETT

N

18. Lake Semerwater

Route: *Lake Semerwater — Stalling Busk — Marsett — Lake Semerwater.*
Distance: *About 4 miles (6.5km). Allow 2½-3 hours. Easy. Field paths and lanes. The route includes one stiff climb, a muddy marshy area and unavoidable road walking.*
O.S. Maps: *Landranger Sheet 98; Outdoor Leisure 30; Hawes footpath map — Stile Publications.*
Parking: *Cars may be parked on the lake foreshore beyond Semerwater Bridge at the north-east side of Lake Semerwater near the Carlow and Mermaid Stones (GR 922876). Car park fee payable.*
Refreshments: *The Stable Tearoom, Countersett — morning coffee, snacks, teas and minerals.*
Note: *Stout footwear essential. A watery walk in wet weather especially between Stalling Busk and Marsett. Lake foreshores are private. All persons using them do so at their own risk. Obey the rules of the Semerwater Sports Association. No public right of way along the banks of Lake Semerwater.*

This Raydale ramble is a delightful little walk which loops the upland lake of Semerwater, which is steeped in superstition and local legend.

The most famous legend of the lake relates to a drowned town beneath its waters, which was sunk by a poor man's curses after he was refused food and drink. Those immortal words are:

"Semer Water rise! Semer Water sink! And swallow all save this lile house that gave me meat and drink."

The Carlow Stone, a huge Shap granite boulder beside Semerwater, is said to be one of the two stones with which the devil and a giant pelted each other from hill to hill across the water.

Another story about the Carlow Stone is that it attracts local couples who are about to marry, because according to superstition it is lucky to touch the stone for prosperity and many children.

Facing the lake, turn left along the lakeland lane for 880 yards to Low Blean Farm and opposite, turn right over the high wooden ladder stile, signposted "Stalling Busk 1 mile", with a request "Please walk in single file — Keep dogs on lead".

From the stile, walk across the pleasant pastures through a series of stiles (three in all with yellow way-marks), and admire the surrounding views including Addlebrough (1,564ft) behind you. Pass a barn on your left, and the signposted route leads you along a muddy path, very close to the lake with no access to the shore.

Beyond the lake, cross not one but two stiles to enter the new Semerwater Nature Reserve — note "The family of Margaret Watson Dale (1909-1986) contributed towards this project in her memory". Gradually climb up the rough pastures on a good path (signposted) through three gated stiles, to reach the ruined church of Stalling Busk (900ft) with access via a slit stile. The old church was built in 1603, rebuilt in 1722 on the same site and abandoned in 1909.

Explore at your own risk, and the churchyard is a peaceful spot with two dozen gravestones, bent at all angles, with one dating back to 1795. From here there are some excellent views of Raydaleside and Semerwater.

From the church, turn right and immediately bear half left (check O.S. map) through a broken wall, and look for a hidden signpost marked "Stalling Busk" (you can easily miss it) which directs you uphill for 880 yards, with a 200-foot stiff climb, above the wooded beckside to the dozen dwellings of the hillside hamlet Stalling Busk (1,100ft).

In Stalling Busk, turn right along the road and bear left to the Church of St Matthew which is well worth a visit, but please secure the church door. This beautiful tiny church (1909) in Swiss village style replaces the ruined church already visited.

Outside the church, bear right to the unsign-posted Busk Lane opposite, where there are splendid views over Raydale into Cragdale and Bardale.

Descend steeply the rough walled lane into Ray-dale and cross a concrete bridge over Cragdale Beck, then turn right alongside the same beck. Continue onwards through a low level area, subject to flooding, so expect plenty of mud.

Cross the footbridge over Raydale Beck, and straight on, cross a slab bridge over Longdale Sike and aim for the stile by a gate. Follow the lane by the embanked Marsett Beck to come out alongside The Green in Marsett, a tiny farming hamlet.

For the return, turn right, cross Marsett Bridge and follow Marsett Lane — normally little traffic except for farm vehicles — for well over a mile. Enjoy the superb views over Semerwater to Stall-ing Busk, and pick out the route already walked.

Well beyond Carr End, as the lane descends, cross the signposted stile on your right and follow the yellow way-marks for 440 yards down the field, and via the wooded beckside to exit through a gate, north of Semerwater Bridge. Return to Lake Semerwater for a perfect finish to a very satisfying short stroll.

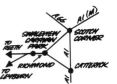

Jockey Cap Clump near Richmond (Walk 10, p42).

Church of St Edmund at Edmundbyers (Walk 26, p104).

Lake Semerwater from Marsett Lane (Walk 18, p66).

The Tees plunges over High Force (Walk 23, p98).

75

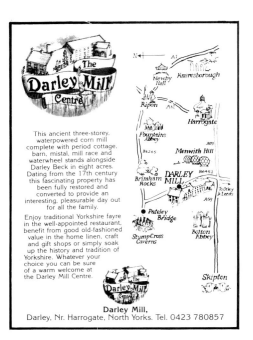

78

Step out on Kielder's self-guided walks!

Whether you're a keen walker or just like a leisurely stroll, you'll love walking at Kielder! We have developed seven different trails for you to enjoy.

See the Romano-British settlement on the Tower Knowe route; the eighteenth century beech trees on Leaplish's Beech Walk; the famous Kielder skew-arch viaduct on the Bakethin North Shore, and the peaceful wooded peninsula around the Belling area.

Our way-marked walks are beautifully described and illustrated in these leaflets available at Tower Knowe and Leaplish Waterside Park, priced 15p.

While you're at Kielder Water, there's plenty more to do ... boardsailing, cycling, fishing, ferry cruising, boating, nature watching ... whatever your interest, you'll love Kielder!

Kielder Water
Northumberland
Tel: (Information Centre) Bellingham (0434) 240398

79

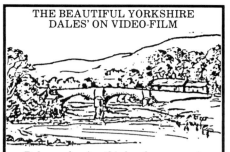

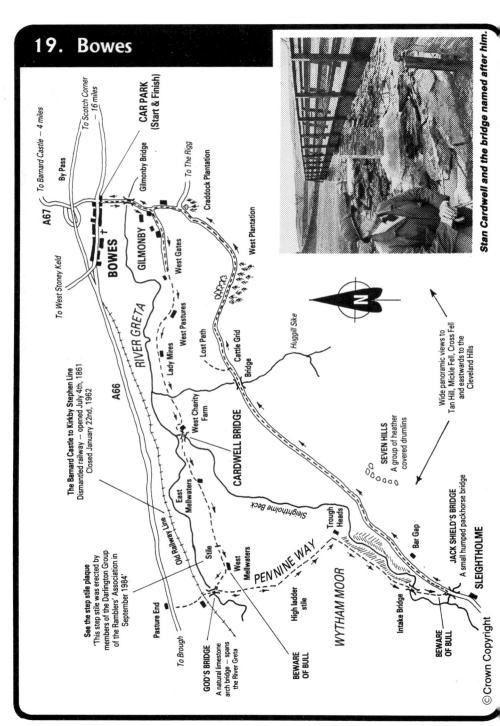

Stan Cardwell and the bridge named after him.

19. Bowes

Route: *Bowes — Gilmonby — Lady Mires — Cardwell Bridge — East Mellwaters — God's Bridge — Intake Bridge — Gilmonby — Bowes.*

Distance: *7½ miles (12km) Allow four hours. Easy to moderate. Field and farm tracks, plus moorland with an elevated road return.*

O.S. Maps: *Landranger Sheet 92; Outdoor Leisure Sheet 30; 1:25,000 Sheet NY91.*

Parking: *Bowes car park. Opposite the village hall, south of the crossroads at the east end of Bowes Village (GR 996135).*

Public Transport: *O.K. Travel: Darlington — Barnard Castle — Carlisle. Check timetables.*

Refreshments: *The Ancient Unicorn Hotel, Bowes (daytime opening hours: Mon — Sat 11am — 3pm; Sunday 12 noon — 3pm).*

Note: *Take particular care during the grouse season.*

The ancient village of Bowes with its castle, church, Roman remains and traditional Dotheboys Hall immortalised by Charles Dickens in Nicholas Nickleby, is the perfect place to start and finish an exploration of Gretadale.

This walk is on flat fields and farm tracks, wild moorland with a stretch of the Pennine Way, and visits five bridges, including the Cardwell Bridge and God's Bridge. The road return is along open moorland with panoramic views.

Before setting out, walk up the village street, pass the Ancient Unicorn Hotel, a sixteenth century coaching inn and visit St Giles Church to see the gravestone of William Shaw, owner/headmaster of Shaw's Academy.

Next to the church, visit Bowes Castle with its Keep built between 1171 and 1187. At the west end of the village is Dotheboys Hall (now in private units), built in the seventeenth century which became the Bowes Academy.

It was visited by Charles Dickens, while collecting material for his book Nicholas Nickleby which illustrated conditions in the notorious Yorkshire Schools.

From Bowes car park, turn left down the road for 440 yards, cross Gilmonby Bridge over the River Greta and enter the hidden hamlet of Gilmonby.

At the road sign "Lady Mires 1 mile", turn right and follow the surfaced No Through Road to pass Gilmonby Farm on your right, the first of six farms en route. Next pass West Gates on your right, then West Pasture on your left and as you walk westwards, admire the backward views to Bowes, dominated by its castle.

After a mile, pass Lady Mires on your left and follow the unsurfaced farm road westwards through a couple of gated fields. As you approach the next farm, look out for the double Pennine Way signpost in the corner wall on your right, which leads you down to West Charity Pasture Farm.

Another similar sign directs you left to the Cardwell Bridge, named after Stanley Cardwell MBE of Darlington, for his contribution to the pleasure of those who look to walk in the countryside. A great tribute to a great walker.

The bridge appears on the recent O.S. Outdoor Leisure Map. Cross the footbridge over Sleightholme Beck and see the stepping stones below.

From the bridge, go between the wall and five trees, walk up the rise and keep by the wall with the River Greta below on your right. Go through the open gateway, bear half left across the field and negotiate the double gates to reach East Mellwaters.

Within the farmyard, turn right, then left by a brick building and left again to pass the sheep collecting pens, and right into a walled lane which heads up the rise.

Keep on this new farm access road, a chipping track and look for the way-marked step stile in the wall, left of a cattle grid.

This stile was erected by members of the Darlington group of the Ramblers' Association in September 1984. Well done, Alan Hutchinson and Anthony Millett. Continue on the access road to West Mellwaters, an old farm built in 1773 and unoccupied for the past 20 years, but at present being renovated.

Beyond the farm, turn half right over the tussock field and watch out for the bull. At the bottom corner of the field, by the old lime kiln, lift up the metal gate to reach the River Greta, which is spanned by a table of limestone, a natural arch known as God's Bridge.

There are views westwards of the wild empty expanse of Stainmore to Tan Hill and beyond. You have now reached the main Pennine Way route, so follow it southwards up the soggy fell pasture and at the top, cross the high ladder stile in the facing wall. Turn left, hug the wall and so far along, turn right over the heather clad Wytham Moor to Trough Heads, an isolated farmstead overlooking the Sleightholme Beck.

Turn right in front of the farm gate, and follow the Pennine Way by the wall on your left until you turn in through a wooden gate (marked Pennine Way on its reverse side). Turn right and follow this ridge path through rushes, high above the Sleightholme Beck.

After passing through a gap in the facing wall, watch out for the path that descends into the valley bottom — you can easily miss it, so check the map.

(Continued on page 84)

83

(Continued from page 83)

Cross Intake Bridge over the beck and walk straight on to straddle the short railed fence. Aim through a gate marked "P. Way" and cut across the final field, but beware of the bull. Exit through the signposted gate out onto the open moorland road, where yards away to your right is a small humped pack horse bridge known as Jack Shields Bridge.

For the return route, turn left along the open moorland road, up past the large farm of Bar Gap to pass the group of heather-covered drumlins on the right of the road known as Seven Hills.

Follow this quiet road, used only by farm traffic, and admire the views to Stainmore, Cross Fell, Mickle Fell and over Gretadale, while eastwards there are fine views to the Cleveland Hills. Follow this road for three miles back to Bowes.

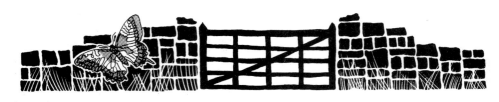

20. Barnard Castle

Route: *Barnard Castle — Flatts Wood — West Holme House — Cotherstone — Mire Lane — Pecknell — Barnard Castle*
Distance: *Over 7 miles (11km). Allow 3-3½ hours. Fairly easy with one steep climb. Riverside, woodland and field paths.*
O.S. Maps: *Landranger Sheet 92; Outdoor Leisure Sheet 31; Pathfinder Sheet NZ01/ 11, NZ02.*
Parking: *Car park, off Galgate, Barnard Castle.*
Public Transport: *United Services and OK Travel serve Barnard Castle. Check timetables.*
Refreshments: *Plenty of pubs, hotels and cafes in Barnard Castle. The Red Lion and The Fox and Hounds, Cotherstone.*

THIS popular Teesdale circular walk from Barnard Castle to Cotherstone is generally regarded as the best riverside and field path ramble around "Barney".

Leave Barnard Castle, go between the Post Office and the Methodist Church at the bottom of Galgate. Go along Scar Top, where the sign "To The Woods" directs you down to Flatts Wood.

Do not cross the Water Bridge but follow the path round to the right and across the footbridge over the Percy Beck. Turn left along the banks of the River Tees through a bramble-covered section of Flatts Wood, where the oak trees were felled by the Raby Estates, some three years ago.

A mile upstream, where the path divides at the rocky stepped outcrops with a yellow way-mark sign, take to the lower route along a narrow path with a steep drop and descend through an attractive stretch of wooded riverside. (The upper path leads you to the remnants of the old Tees Valley railway viaduct.)

Further on, follow the path uphill (ignore the track on your right) and admire the views across the river to Towler Hill Farm. Go down to the riverside and along the well-known Rock Walk, created by Dr George Edwards well over a century ago, with permission of the Earl of Darlington.

You will pass between two large moss-covered boulders called the Wishing Stones and, providing you don't touch them, your wish will be granted. Continue along the water's edge by the overhanging cliffs and climb up the stone staircase of 29 steps, with the sign "Danger — Beware of Falling Rocks". Back in the wood, turn left along the muddy riverside path and the moss-covered ruined wall on your left is part of the old deer park.

Continue for 880 yards (ignore the track to the right) and exit out of the wood through a way-marked wooden gate into a large pasture called Heslop's Bottom. Proceed straight on, hug the wall/wood on your right for 100 yards and turn right through a way-marked gate for a steep climb up through the wood and at the top, cross a stile into the open fields.

Turn left along the edge of the gated/stiled fields above the wood and in the second full field, with

the whitewashed East Holme House away to your right, watch out for the Electric Shepherd — a single electric battery unit. Follow the way-marks round and down through a gate to pass in front of West Holme House, another whitewashed farmstead. Beyond the farm, go through a couple of way-marked gated fields and in the third, curve round and follow the white and yellow arrows to cross step stile on your left.

Descend the narrow, slippery path into the wooded gill, cross the slabstone footbridge and uphill, go through the gate in the facing wall. Proceed straight on and turn right in front of a gate (do not go through) and follow the path by the wall over the next three stile/gated fields. Look for a stone wall stile on your left and follow the wooded path down to the pleasant riverside pastures. Cross the footbridges over the Tees and Balder, noting where these rivers meet.

Here you can either go right to reach Cotherstone along the tarmac path by the natural amphitheatre of The Hagg, with a climb up to this delightful village with a couple of pleasant pubs, or climb the steep, stepped path directly in front of you, up the mound of the old Cotherstone Castle.

At the top, turn left, go through a metal gate, pass between the hen crees and a timber building to cross a stile on your left. Walk along the elevated path, where you will unexpectedly be confronted by the isolated grave of Abraham Hilton, one of the best-known "Sons of Teesdale".

From the grave, join the farm road from The Mill and follow this via Demesne Lane to come out opposite the school in Cotherstone. Turn left along the main street (B6277) and beyond Meadowcroft, turn left again (public footpath signposted) into Mire Lane.

Follow this enclosed lane through a facing wooden gate and out in the open field, look for a stile in the short wall on your right at the end of the field, go through a corner squeeze stile. So far up the next field, cross a way-marked stile by a holly bush and turn acutely right up the field to cross a way-marked stile in the facing fence. Bear half left,

(Continued on page 87)

85

20. Barnard Castle

N

BARNARD CASTLE
An Historic Market Town
Gateway to Teesdale
(Start & Finish)

THE ROCK WALK
One of three well known walks in Flatts Wood, created by Dr George Edwards, with permission from the Earl of Darlington, over a century ago

WISHING STONES
Two moss covered boulders. Pass through them without touching and you wish will be granted

WATCH OUT FOR THE ELECTRIC SHEPHERD
A single electric battery unit

DANGER BEWARE OF FALLING ROCKS

Stone
Staircase of
29 steps

FLATTS WOOD
Stone buttress ends of the demolished Tees Valley viaduct

Percy Beck

Post Office

Galgate

Castle

Scar
Top

A67

To Bowes

DEEPDALE AQUEDUCT
or Water-Bridge built in 1893. It is 160ft in length and 20ft high

Pecknell Wood

B6277

Follow yellow arrows

East Holme House

Steep Climb

West Holme House

Follow the white and yellow waymark arrows

Slab bridge

Follow yellow waymarks

See the solitary grave of Abraham Hilton — the Teesdale Philanthropist known as "Old Abey Hilton".

Meeting of the Waters
where the River Balder and Tees meet

RIVER TEES

Dismantled Railway

Pecknell

Scur Beck

Grise Beck
Wood

Cooper
House

Mire Lane

Stile

Grise Beck

Stile

**Beware
of Bull**

LARTINGTON

Lartington Hall
built in the reign of Charles I

TEESDALE

F.B.

To Romaldkirk

Balder Bridge

RIVER BALDER

COTHERSTONE

To Bowes

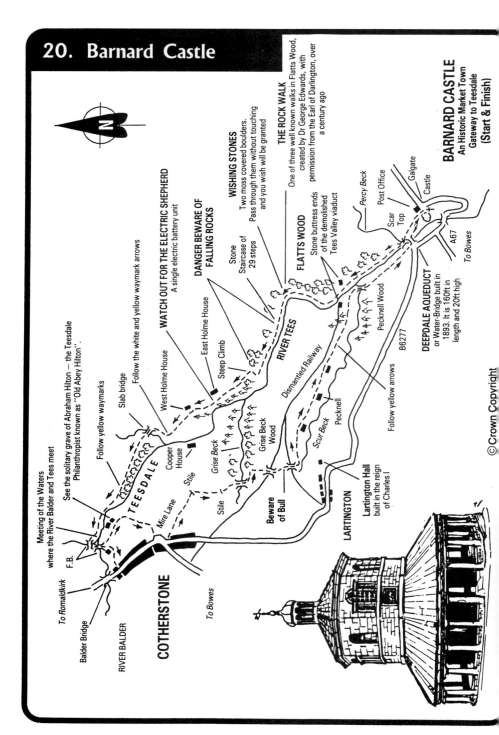

(Continued from page 85)

aim for the corner of Grise Beck Wood, cross the cart bridge and keep the wood on your left.

At the end of the same field, turn right in front of the gate and follow the path over the gated bridge across the disused Barnard Castle/Middleton railway line.

Continue straight on over the next field and watch out for the grazing bull. Go under the old bridge of the Barnard Castle/Bowes railway line and aim for the gate, across a field, with a dozen small crees. Turn left along the track by the boundary wall of Lartington Park, with its impressive

Lartington Hall. Go through a white gate, past a nearby cottage and follow the field path to Pecknell Farm with its tall barn and unusual date stone of 1866.

From the farm, pass behind an isolated house and follow the way-marks fixed on the telegraph poles to go through a white gate into Pecknell Wood, where the track is very muddy.

Join a broad cart road downhill, pass the restored Tees Bank Cottage and follow the bridle track for 880 yards to reach the B6277 road. Turn left and left again to cross the Deepdale Aqueduct over the River Tees and retrace your steps back to Barnard Castle.

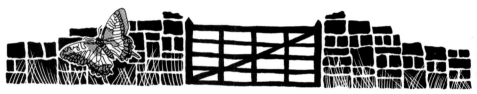

21. Barnard Castle

SCAR TOP
(START & FINISH)

BARNARD CASTLE
Historic market town.
Gateway to Teesdale.

Bowes Museum

School

Demesne

Castle

Gogye

County Bridge

Caravan Park

Thorsgill Beck

Abbey Lane

To A66

Thorngate Bridge
(Closed for repairs)

Alternative path

Teesdale —
"The undiscovered corner of England"

To Whorlton

Mains House Farm

Stiles missing

Tees Bank Plantation

Map navigation needed

Meeting of the Waters —
where the River Greta joins
the River Tees

Steep path

Sledwich Gill

Follow yellow arrows
through waymarked stiles

West Thorpe
a roofless ruined barn

WHORLTON
A lovely village with
a large green

To A67

+

To A66

WHORLTON BRIDGE
A suspension bridge
built in 1831

WHORLTON LIDO
A popular riverside
recreation area

Follow yellow arrows
through waymarked stiles

MORTHAM TOWER
A 15th century fortified
farmhouse — a former
peel tower

River Tees

DAIRY BRIDGE
Turner painted a
watercolour study of
this ivy clad bridge
in 1820

River Greta

To A66

ROKEBY PARK
An 18th century
country house

Manyfold Beck

PARADISE WALK
A mile long wooded
riverside path

ABBEY BRIDGE
A farmer toll bridge,
60ft high with a
span of 75ft
built in 1773

BOW BRIDGE
A 17th Century —
Packhorse Bridge

EGGLESTONE ABBEY
A picturesque 12th century
ruined abbey

N

© Crown Copyright

88

21. Barnard Castle

Route: *Barnard Castle — County Bridge — Egglestone Abbey — Abbey Bridge — The Meeting of the Waters — Whorlton — Sledwich Gill — Mains House Farm — Demesne — Barnard Castle.*
Distance: *Under 9 miles (14.5km). Fairly easy, all field walk. Allow 4/5 hours.*
O.S. Maps: *Landranger Sheet 92; Pathfinder Sheet NZ01/11*
Public Transport: *United Services, OK Travel from Darlington and Bishop Auckland.*
Refreshments: *Pubs, hotels and cafes in Barnard Castle; The Bridge Inn, Whorlton.*

This riverside ramble between Barnard Castle and Whorlton packs into its nine miles, some of the finest riverside scenery in Teesdale.

Its main attractions are a pack horse bridge, a picturesque abbey, a pele tower, plus the popular Paradise Walk and the Meeting of the Waters.

From the historic market town of Barnard Castle, leave Galgate between the Post Office and Trinity Methodist Church to Scar Top Park. Go down by the castle and beneath this historic ruin, cross the County Bridge (1569) and turn left along the B6277 for the best backward views of the bridge and castle.

Just before the Z road sign, turn left along the wooded riverside to Thorngate Bridge and go up the steep railed path and left along The Lendings, where at its end, go through the gated stile and up through the caravan park. Climb the tarmac road and cross the way-marked wooden stile in the fence on your left.

Proceed eastwards along the next four fields, stiled and way-marked with yellow arrows. There are excellent views over the Tees to Bowes Museum and Barnard Castle School.

Exit through a stone stile into Abbey Lane and 200 yards down this narrow lane is Bow Bridge, a seventeenth century pack horse bridge. Here you get your first glimpse of Egglestone Abbey. Continue along Abbey Lane and visit the remains of Egglestone Abbey founded by Ralph de Multon in 1195 for the Premonstatensian canons. Rejoin the lane and follow this 440 yards to Abbey Bridge, a former toll bridge built by John Sawley Morritt and opened in 1773.

To shorten the route, walk over the bridge and turn left through the wall gap and follow the path for a riverside return to Barnard Castle.

For the main walk, take the path on the south, right hand side of the bridge, go through a new gate and follow the winding gravel path down to the Tees with excellent views of Abbey Bridge.

This mile-long wooded riverside path, known locally as Paradise Walk has always been a firm favourite with generations of walkers, especially for its magnificent riverside scenery.

Where the gravel path ends, go down to the rocky river edge and watch out for the high nettles. Cross Manyfold Beck for a stiff climb and at the top of the field, continue eastwards to enter another stretch of woodland, with some more high vegetation. You come out into Mortham lane and turn left

along this for a half mile, noting Rokeby Park, an eighteenth century country house.

You will reach the popular scenic spot, known as the Meeting of the Waters, where the Greta joins the Tees, which has inspired poet and artist alike. It was here that Joseph Turner made a watercolour study of Dairy Bridge and Sir Walter Scott wrote his 30,000-word poem Rokeby. Cross Dairy Bridge and follow the driveway marked "Mortham Tower — Please keep to the footpath" in the direction of Mortham Tower, a fifteenth century pele tower or fortified farmhouse built, as a protection against the Scots.

As the driveway curves right, turn left and aim for a way-marked stile in the fence. Cross this and walk eastwards along the edge of the next two way-marked stiled fields. In the third field, curve left by the potato field and follow the track along the same field with the wall on your left.

Pass the roofless ruin of West Thorpe and go through the corner gap and along the field edge by the wall with high thistles. Exit through a way-marked gate and diagonally half left over a final pasture to come out opposite the well-known Whorlton Lido, a leisure recreation park.

Turn left and cross Whorlton Bridge, a suspension bridge, 32 feet high with a span of 180 feet which was started in August 1830 and completed in July 1831. By the toll cottage, climb the steep steps up to the picturesque village of Whorlton with its lovely green and secluded church. The Bridge Inn provides refreshments.

For the return, turn left at the top of the steps by the sign Whorlton and follow the signposted footpath along the top of the wooded Whorlton Banks, by the gardens of Whorlton Court and Riverside. Go through a corner gate and head westwards along the edge of the next four gated/stiled fields with the wood on your left. Down an enclosed path, and out through a rusty gate. Keep straight on by a line of old oak trees and veer left down to a way-marked blue gate. Now follow the path westwards by the wood and along the stiled fields.

When you see the Public Footpath sign, cross the stile and follow the path within the woodland edge that leads to the narrow ravine of Sledwich Gill. Go steeply down the steps, ford the gill and ascend the narrow path with a steep drop and negotiate this tricky path with overhanging nettles. At

(Continued on page 90)

(Continued from page 89)

the top, cross the stone wall stile and continue along the next four gated/stiled fields. Cross a double stile, veer right and hug the stone wall, where at the end of the field, cross a stone wall stile and aim half left over the next field for a similar stile. Bear half left again and aim for a corner stile above Tees Bank Plantation.

Follow the path eastwards through three fields with stiles missing, so straddle the field fences with care. Bear left down to the corner gate and along the field by the wall and go through a stone wall stile shielded by a rusty metal gate. You drop down to the road and turn up this until it swings right by a wooden seat and turn left through a way-marked kissing gate.

There is a superb view over the Tees to Egglestone Abbey. Follow the well-used path through the stiled fields and diagonally over the popular Demesne, with detailed direction not necessary, although you might encounter some drainage works in Parsons Lonnen, as you return to Barnard Castle.

Low water at Cow Green Reservoir (Walk 24, p100).

Spectacular views from near Sutton Bank (Walk 6, p17).

The Hole of Horcum from a point near Levisham (Walk 3, p10).

God's Bridge spans the River Greta (Walk 19, p82).

22. Stanhope

Route: Stanhope — Stanhope Dene — Stanhope Burn Mine — Crawley Incline — Crawley Edge — Linkirk Cave — Stanhope.

Distance: Over 8 miles (13km) or about 6 miles (9.5km). Allow 4/5 hours. Moderate/fairly strenuous. Woodland, waterfalls, mines, moor and meadow.

O.S. Maps: Landranger Sheets 92 and 87.

Parking: Market Place, Stanhope.

Public Transport: Weardale Service 101/102, Bishop Auckland — Stanhope.

Refreshments: The Bonny Moor Hen; Coffee Mill; Chatters; The Pack Horse Hotel; Sandwich Bar; The Grey Bull; The Queen's Head. None on route.

Warning: Do not explore the mines — they are dangerous. Keep out of the old quarries with deep pools. Map and compass essential. Do not attempt in doubtful weather. Expect plenty of mud with slippery paths.

This walk reveals the varied delights and dangers of Weardale — mines, quarries, old railway lines and the cave of the little people.

Leave Stanhope by walking west along the A689 or from the Market Place, turn down The Butts and walk along the tree-lined riverside, known locally as the Wear Walk. Go up to the Memorial Fountain and turn left along the A689.

Beyond Burnside House (1905), cross the Stanhope Burn Bridge and before Stanhope Hall, a twelfth century fortified manor house (now a hotel and restaurant), turn right into the enclosed lane (public footpath signposted). Follow this northwards, pass the Mill, go through the open gateway and bear right before the caravans and left along the wooded Stanhope Burn.

Keep by the burn, ignore the footbridge and climb the perimeter woodland path, which becomes fenced, with direction not needed. When you see a yellow arrow way-mark on a gate post (it is misleading), do not go through the adjacent wooden gate, but walk on and turn right through a rusty metal gate and follow the enclosed path uphill.

Cross a four-plank bridge and re-enter the wooded valley of Stanhope Dene. Follow this woodland path uphill (very muddy) and when it splits, take the lower route which crosses a couple of footbridges and leads you down to the Stanhope Burn. Cross the footbridge over the burn and climb steeply out of the valley via a series of steps up to the quarry road. Turn left along this road for 880 yards, past the bygone lead mining and quarrying industry of Weardale, including the deep pools of West Pasture Quarry and arched entrances of old lead mine levels. Remember these are unsafe and dangerous, do not explore.

Stride out along the valley quarry road, until at the Stanhope Burn Mine, you see past and present activity of the lead mining industry. Beyond the Hymac digger, turn right and then left up the stony track and exit through a metal gate out on to the moor. The track swings uphill by the stone wall, with views back down Stanhope Dene and over the Heathery Burn, famed for its Bronze Age finds of 1872.

St Thomas's Church, Stanhope

Continue to climb and where the wall turns right downhill, the moorland trail becomes a short turf track, known as the Velvet Path. Follow this for a further 440 yards to cross the B6278 to reach the old Stanhope and Tyne Valley Railway. As shown on my map, it is possible to make a moorland extension of a mile up to the site of the Weatherill Engine, part of the Stanhope and Tyne Railway.

The route, a public right of way, leaves the Velvet Path opposite the fourth transmission pole on your right and before the old British Railway wagon, turn left up a small gulley, then northeastwards up a pathless moor of tussock grass and heather to come out at Weatherill cottages. Opposite, head southwards down the disused Stanhope and Tyne Valley Railway for 1½ miles, noting the old marker stones inscribed with "S & D.R".

This old mineral line linked Weardale with Tynedale from Crawleyside to Weatherill and Parkhead to South Shields. Walk south down the wagonway parallel to the B6278 to join the shorter route and pass the redundant Crawley Reservoir, noting all the time the wide views of Weardale. Leave the walkway, as you approach a partially renovated house, turn left along a track and once through the gate posts, turn right by the garden wall of the same house. Follow the track and veer left, eastwards along Crawley Edge (about 1,000ft).

Keep on the broad path for a mile, skirting above Ashes Quarry and when the path splits, bear right

(Continued on page 97)

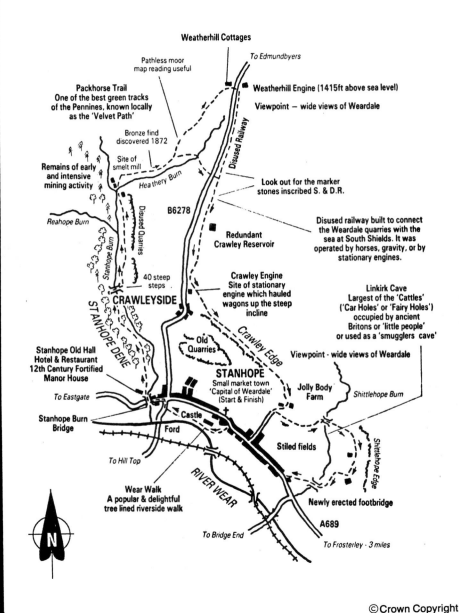

Weatherhill Cottages

To Edmundbyers

Pathless moor
map reading useful

Weatherhill Engine (1415ft above sea level)

Viewpoint — wide views of Weardale

Packhorse Trail
One of the best green tracks
of the Pennines, known locally
as the 'Velvet Path'

Disused Railway

Bronze find
discovered 1872

Site of
smelt mill

Look out for the marker
stones inscribed S. & D.R.

Remains of early
and intensive
mining activity

Heathery Burn

Reahope Burn

Disused Quarries

Stanhope Burn

B6278

Redundant
Crawley Reservoir

Disused railway built to connect
the Weardale quarries with the
sea at South Shields. It was
operated by horses, gravity, or by
stationary engines.

40 steep
steps

CRAWLEYSIDE

Crawley Engine
Site of stationary
engine which hauled
wagons up the steep
incline

Linkirk Cave
Largest of the 'Cattles'
('Car Holes' or 'Fairy Holes')
occupied by ancient
Britons or 'little people'
or used as a 'smugglers cave'

STANHOPE DENE

Old
Quarries

Crawley Edge

Viewpoint - wide views of Weardale

Stanhope Old Hall
Hotel & Restaurant
12th Century Fortified
Manor House

STANHOPE
Small market town
'Capital of Weardale'
(Start & Finish)

Jolly Body
Farm

Shittlehope Burn

To Eastgate

Stanhope Burn
Bridge

Castle

Ford

Stiled fields

Shittlehope Edge

To Hill Top

Wear Walk
A popular & delightful
tree lined riverside walk

RIVER WEAR

Newly erected footbridge

A689

To Bridge End

To Frosterley - 3 miles

N

Continued from page 95)

below a walled enclosure and beyond a small woodland, turn right downhill and left along a track by Craig Cottage and over a stile to come out opposite Jolly Boddy Farm. Turn down the lane and if you wish to shorten the walk, follow it all the way down to Stanhope.

Otherwise, look out for a laneside cottage called Isengard on your right and cross a public footpath signposted stile on your left. Now follow the path eastwards over four stiled fields and once over a partially white-painted ladder stile, bear right to cross a stile and down the wooded beckside path to cross a one-railed footbridge over the Shittlehope Burn.

Here, look downstream to see the Linkirk Cave, largest of the Cattles (Cat Holes or Fairy Holes) in the area. The cave is said to have been occupied by ancient Britons, the 'little people' and used as a smugglers' cave. Climb the stepped path out of the wooded ravine, cross a stile and bear half right over the field to squeeze through a fallen white-painted gate. Turn left up the field and pass between ruined Ravensfield farmhouse and onwards over the field to cross a short railed fence by an empty house.

Turn right down the watery meadow and right past a farm entrance to cross a facing stile into a watery sunken lane, with hawthorn bushes on either side. Head down this lane — most walkers seem to have used the outside — which turns down to cross a newly-erected footbridge over the Shittlehope Burn. Follow the path along a final field to go between the bungalows called Kimberley and Vindorn, turn left down Woodcroft Gardens to the A689 to come out opposite Weardale Motors. Turn right along the main road, back to Stanhope.

Durham County Council
BOWLEES PICNIC AREA
Gibson's Cave Nature Trial
Footpath by permission of
Raby Estates
(Start and Finish)

GIBSON'S CAVE
No access beyond this
point. Follow yellow
waymarks

Summerhill Force

Newbiggin Methodist Chapel
1759
This is the oldest chapel in
Methodism to have held services
continuously since it was built.
A pulpit used by John Wesley within

NEWBIGGIN

To Middleton-in-Teesdale

BEWARE
OF
BULL

BOWLEES

Bowlees Beck

Scoberry Bridge

PENNINE WAY
England's oldest
long distance
footpath

TEESDALE'S OLD ROAD
Forest to Middleton
main road until 1820
now a Public Bridleway.
Please close all gates

Smithy Sike

Ash Hill

Etters Gill Beck

TEESDALE

Low Force
or
Salmon Leap

High Force Hotel

Holwick
Head Bridge

NOTICE
Livestock at risk.
Dogs must be on a lead,
these fields are not for
recreation, please keep
to footpath

WYNCH BRIDGE
Nicknamed the "Two Inch Bridge".
Present suspension bridge replaces
earlier bridge built in 1704 — said
to be the first suspension bridge in
Europe. This bridge is to carry ordinary
foot traffic and should be used by
one person at a time.

Picnic Area
Car Park

TEES

Persons visiting High Force
do so at their own risk.
Visitors are warned to
keep to the paths

RIVER

HIGH FORCE
England's largest
waterfall

N

23. Bowlees

Route: *Bowlees — Ash Hill — Dirt Pit — High Force — Holwick Head Bridge — Wynch Bridge — Scoberry Bridge — Newbiggin — Bowlees.*
Distance: *Over 5 miles (8km). Fairly easy. Allow 3 to 3½ hours including visit to Bowlees Visitors' Centre and High Force.*
O.S. Maps: *Landranger Sheet 92; Pathfinder Sheet NY82/92; Outdoor Leisure Sheet 31.*
Public Transport: *United Service 76 from Barnard Castle to Bowlees.*
Parking: *Bowlees Car Park, near Newbiggin in Teesdale GR907283. Heed the police warnings. Take valuables with you.*
Refreshments: *High Force Hotel.*
Warning: *Heed the notices displayed within Bowlees Picnic Area and at High Force.*

This is the finest waterfall walk in England, with three famous falls to see on this short stroll through Upper Teesdale.

This walk starts and ends at the award-winning Bowlees Picnic Area where within, follow the Nature Trail upstream and see the spectacular Summerhill Force tumbling over Gibson's Cave, the hiding place of a sixteenth century outlaw.

Return to the Picnic Area, cross Bowlees Beck and follow the path for 100 yards to Bowlees Visitors' Centre. The centre explains the history and life of past and present Teesdale.

Pass in front of the Centre, walk forward and go through the facing gate signposted public bridleway and follow the gated track uphill (closing all gates). The second gate is marked Beware of the Bull so walk with care. This was Teesdale's main road from Forest to Middleton until 1820. At the top you will pass the whitewashed farmhouse of Ash Hill, 1,105 feet above sea level, which offers extensive views. From here, it is downhill for a while to the farm cottages of Dirt Pit meaning Deerpeth, where the monks of Rievaulx Abbey maintained a chapel for the forest keepers.

Go between the cottages, cross the bridge over Ettersgill Road where opposite, cross the signposted stile into a watery meadow. Detour round the swampy area, aim diagonally uphill and go through a gate by a small whitewashed barn. Go straight over the next field, through another gate, turn left and cross the corner signposted stile into the picnic area at High Force.

The High Force Hotel is the ideal halfway house for refreshments. Opposite pay your admission for a woodland walk to see High Force — England's largest waterfall. Here the Tees plunges 70 feet over the Great Whin Sill. Please heed the warnings.

Back at the B6277 turn down the road with no footway for 600 yards and then right down a wooded track marked Private Road — No Access for Vehicles. Do not be deterred, it is a public right of way. Cross Holwick Head Bridge over the Tees.

You have now joined the Pennine Way, England's oldest long distance walk. Turn downstream and although detailed direction is not necessay for a couple of miles, you are reminded to keep to the paths and keep dogs under control. With the Tees as your companion, follow the stiled path by some of the best riverside scenery in the country.

After a mile you will reach the Salmon Leap, better known as Low Force or Little Force. Below this waterfall is Wynch Bridge, a chain suspension bridge nicknamed the Two Inch Bridge which replaced an earlier bridge built in 1704, said to have been the first suspension bridge in Europe. To shorten the walk, cross this elegant chain bridge one person at a time and follow the path through the wood and over a couple of stiled fields for a quick return to Bowlees.

For a longer walk, follow the Pennine Way for some 880 yards and en route cross a footbridge with nearby medieval mines. This route is noted for its wild flowers and variety of bird life during spring and summer.

Leave the Pennine Way, by crossing the slender Scoberry Bridge over the Tees, bear half right over the field, aim for a black barn and go through the adjacent gate. In the next field bear half right again and cross the footbridge over the Bowlees Beck. Turn up the walled path, cross a stile and turn half right over the field to exit over a stile on to the B6277. Turn right into Newbiggin. Pass the village hall and outside Rose Cottage Farm, cross the road and walk up the village lane to Newbiggin Chapel. Turn left along the road past Fellowship Farm on your left and uphill, take the signposted path through the stile by the gate on your left.

You will encounter plenty of mud over the next two way-marked stiled fields, to pass behind the terraced cottages of Hood Gill. Continue by the field edge, go through a way-marked gate, and through the centre of the next field turn down the track back to Bowlees Picnic Area.

N

To Alston

Alternative Start

B6277

To Middleton-in-Teesdale

LANGDON BECK HOTEL

Harwood Beck

GRAZING STOCK
All dogs must be
on a lead

**Upper Teesdale National
Nature Reserve**
boundary signpost

Signpost – 'Cauldron Snout 3½ miles'

R I V E R   T E E S

To Harwood

Peghorn Lane

Join the Pennine Way

Widdybank Farm
Tea, coffee & snacks

Cronkley Scar

C R O N K L E Y   F E L L

**WIDDYBANK FELL
NATURE TRAIL START**
— Total distance
5km – 3 miles
allow 2 hours

W I D D Y B A N K   F E L L

N A T U R E   T R A I L

Kissing Gate with
wheelchair access

• **Weather station**

Please keep to the footpath

P E N N I N E   W A Y

Rocky riverside path
strewn with large boulders.
Boulder hopping/scramble.

**WHEELHEAD SIKE
CAR PARK**
GR 810309
START & FINISH

C O U N T Y   D U R H A M

CAULDRON SNOUT
One of the most
impressive waterfalls
in Britain (steep climb)

Falcon Clints

Follow the path along
a series of duck boards

COW GREEN RES.
Opened by Alderman
J S Dyball, Chairman
of the Board, on
July 22, 1971

C U M B R I A

COW GREEN DAM
Constructed 1967 to 1970
Length of dam – 1,875 ft.
height of dam – 82 ft.
Area of reservoir – 770 acres

Pennine Way to
Birkdale

Maize Beck

Where the
Maize Beck joins
the River Tees.
The County Boundary
between Cumbria and
County Durham

24. Cow Green

Route: *Weelhead Sike car park — Peghorn Lane — Widdybank Farm — Falcon Clints — Cauldron Snout — Weelhead Sike car park.*

Distance: *8 miles (12.8km). Moderate/strenuous. Allow 5 hrs. A lot of road walking plus the surfaced nature trail. Boulder-hopping and steep scramble.*

O.S. Maps: *Landranger Sheets 92 or 91; Outdoor Leisure Sheet 31.*

Parking: *Weelhead Sike car park at the end of Peghorn Lane, three miles west of Langdon Beck (GR 810309). Warning — car thieves operate in this area.*

Refreshments: *Langdon Beck Hotel; Widdybank Farm — tea, coffee and snacks.*

Note: *Weather conditions can quickly change in Upper Teesdale. Be prepared for the worst, as conditions in winter can be Arctic. Walkers should be properly equipped with waterproof clothing and walking boots. Map and compass essential.*

Stretch your legs with this walk on the wild side in Upper Teesdale. Although this short tour is only eight miles, it is a tough little trek that ought not to be taken lightly and should command respect from even the most ardent of walkers. Using part of the Pennine Way, it takes you along the River Tees to Cauldron Snout, one of the finest waterfalls in England, and returns with a Nature Trail finish.

This circuit is best done in a clockwise direction, especially for the surprise view of Cauldron Snout. You may prefer to start at Langdon Beck and finish with a downhill road walk, or if you're lucky to have a transport manager, you can be dropped off at the entrance to Widdybank Farm road and collected at Weelhead Sike car park. The Nature Trail gives the quickest and most direct route to Cauldron Snout, a there-and-back, two hour walk of three miles.

Start from Weelhead Sike car park and walk back down Peghorn Lane for 2½ miles noting the down dale vista of Upper Teesdale. Pass a white-washed barn on your left, cross a cattle grid and turn right to the open gateway with a notice stating "Grazing Stock — all dogs must be on a lead." The farm entrance road is signed "Cauldron Snout Fall."

Follow the winding farm road into the National Nature Reserve with a second sign indicating "Cauldron Snout 3½ miles". Admire the impressive views of Upper Teesdale dotted with the whitewashed farmsteads of the Raby Estate.

Soon Cronkley Scar comes into view with its high, dark cliffs dominating the surrounding scenery. Follow the rough farm road and a further directional sign on a breeze block barn indicates "Cauldron Snout 2 miles" — it seems more than two miles when walking into a head-on wintry wind of rain and sleet. A mile from Peghorn Lane, you reach the isolated, whitewashed Widdybank Farm which offers tea, coffee and snacks.

You have now joined the Pennine Way, the second longest footpath in Britain. Pass through the gated farmyard, follow the Pennine Way signs along a gravel track, and cross the corner wall stile, the only one on the entire walk. Follow the path by the River Tees along the pleasant green pastures of Holmwath with the sloping heights of Widdybank Fell (1,762ft) away up to your right.

You will encounter a short section of duck boarding, as the walk follows the riverside edge for a scramble over slippery, large boulders. Great care must be exercised on this section of path. In fact, you might find that you have to use all fours along this rocky riverside. Further on, there is a long stretch of more duck boarding as you skirt below the impressive high cliffs of Falcon Clints.

With more boulder-hopping you round the riverside to reach the confluence of the River Tees and Maize Beck, which was the meeting place of the counties of Yorkshire, Durham and Westmorland — today the boundary between Durham and Cumbria.

Eventually you reach the highlight of the walk, England's finest waterfall, Cauldron Snout, with the Tees cascading 200 feet over the Great Whin Sill. Take the path on the east side of the waterfall for a steep scramble up the well-worn rocky outcrops. Great care must be taken when climbing this path which can be slippery and muddy in wet weather.

At the top of the falls, look back for a view of Durham's highest summit, Mickle Fell (2,591ft), while ahead of you is the impressive dam head of Cow Green Reservoir opened in 1971.

To complete the walk, turn right along the surfaced Nature Trail (please keep to the path) and follow this northwards for 1½ miles, with excellent views of Cow Green Reservoir to the Pennine summits of Knock Fell, Great Dun Fell, Little Dun Fell and Cross Fell.

Exit through the kissing gate, leave the nature reserve, turn left along the road and then right up a gravel path — once a miners' tramway for conveying barytes from the nearby disused lead mines — and return to the car park.

25. Wolsingham

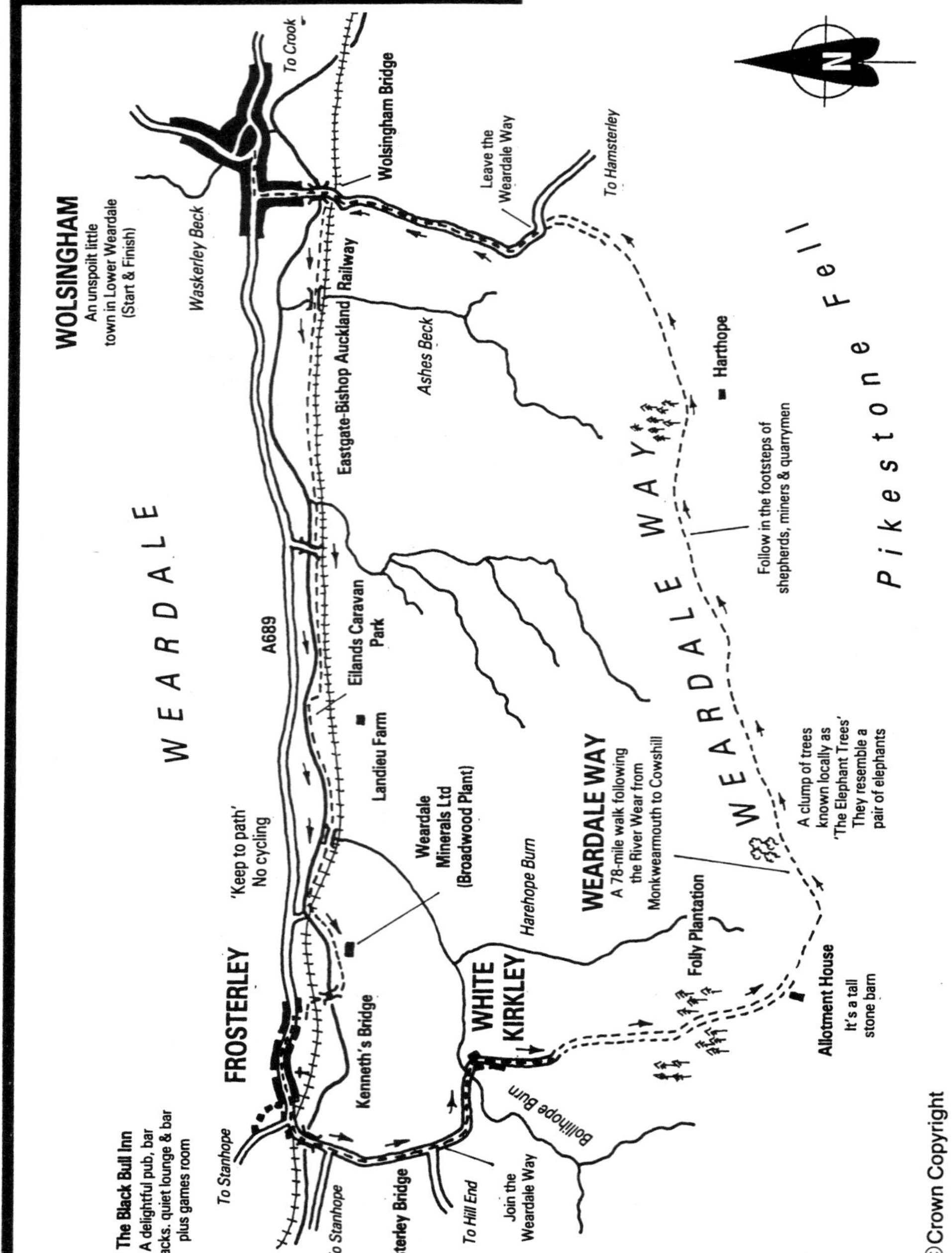

WOLSINGHAM
An unspoilt little town in Lower Weardale (Start & Finish)

To Crook

Wolsingham Bridge

Waskerley Beck

Leave the Weardale Way

To Hamsterley

Eastgate-Bishop Auckland Railway

Ashes Beck

Harthope

P i k e s t o n e   F e l l

W E A R D A L E

A689

Ellands Caravan Park

Landieu Farm

Follow in the footsteps of shepherds, miners & quarrymen

'Keep to path' No cycling

Weardale Minerals Ltd (Broadwood Plant)

Harehope Burn

W
E
A
R
D
A
L
E
 W
A
Y

A clump of trees known locally as 'The Elephant Trees'. They resemble a pair of elephants

FROSTERLEY

Kenneth's Bridge

WHITE KIRKLEY

WEARDALE WAY
A 78-mile walk following the River Wear from Monkwearmouth to Cowshill

Folly Plantation

Allotment House
It's a tall stone barn

The Black Bull Inn
A delightful pub, bar snacks, quiet lounge & bar plus games room

To Stanhope

To Stanhope

Frosterley Bridge

To Hill End

Join the Weardale Way

Bollihope Burn

102

25. Wolsingham

Route: Wolsingham — Frosterley — White Kirkley — Allotment House — Elephant Trees — Wear Bank — Wolsingham.
Distance: About 10 miles (16km). Moderate. Allow 5/6 hours. Easy to follow.
O.S. Maps: Landranger Sheet 92; 1:25,000 First Series Sheet NZ 03; Outdoor Leisure Sheet 31.
Parking: Market Place, Wolsingham.
Public Transport: Weardale Motor Services, Service 102, Bishop Auckland — Stanhope.
Refreshments: The Black Bull, Pegotty's Cafe, The Beehive, The Grey Bull Hotel, Wolsingham; The Frosterley Inn; The Black Bull Inn, Frosterley.

This walk is one of the best in the Durham Dales and deserves to be better known. A ten-mile round trip from Wolsingham, it uses pleasant field and riverside paths to the village of Frosterley and returns along the moor edge of Pikestone Fell for a bracing walk, with extensive views over Weardale.

Leave Wolsingham by walking west along Front Street (A689) and at the road sign "Hamsterley 5 miles" turn left along the Causeway and cross Wolsingham Bridge over the River Wear. Turn right up the road for 20 yards to the public footpath sign on your right and go through the gap in the wall, down the 22 steps to follow the fenced path between the railway and wooded riverside.

Onwards, cross a footbridge over Ashes Beck and proceed west along the pastures, keeping by the fenced railside. Cross a further footbridge over Hole Beck to join the River Wear. Turn upstream by the wooded riverside and look out for herons. Cross another footbridge by the weir to come out by the road bridge over the river. Continue straight on through an open way-marked gateway, with the sign "Landieu Farm". Follow the surfaced farm road and although detailed direction is not necessary for the next 880 yards, the notice "Ellands Caravan Park — Private No Through Road" reminds you that the land and riverbank is private property, so keep to the roadway.

When you reach the caravan park entrance, a footpath sign directs you into the site and past a bungalow, where a second footpath sign fixed on an ash tree near the river, points the way upstream by a low hawthorn hedge. At the end of the caravan park, ignore the stile on your left and walk forward to cross the footbridge over Bollihope Beck. Follow the field path with a request "Keep to the path — No Cycling" and note the white way-marks on the trees to exit through a little gate out onto the road. Turn left and over the railway crossing, turn right into Broadwood plant of Weardale Minerals. Here you encounter the Wear Valley Way, a long-distance footpath from Killhope Wheel to Willington.

Beyond the car park and office cabins, at the public footpath sign, turn right, cross the stile and climb up the narrow wooded path above the River Wear. Follow this path, fenced and way-marked by the old quarry works, and bear right down through a way-marked gate following the path to the riverside. Cross the long wooden bridge known as Kenneth's Bridge over the Wear. Cross also, the railway line and follow the unmade road into the village of Frosterley, famous for its Black Limestone marble, used to build part of Durham Cathedral.

If you wish to shorten the walk, you can catch the hourly bus back to Wolsingham.

Opposite the Frosterley Inn, turn left along the main street (A689), where St Michael's Church with its tall spire makes an interesting detour. At the west end of the village, turn left down the lane signposted "White Kirkley 1 mile" to a pleasant pub called the Black Bull Inn.

From the pub, cross Frosterley Bridge, pass through Bridge End and walk up the road for 880 yards, noting the derelict quarry workings reclaimed by nature. At the road junction, join the Weardale Way, pioneered by Ken Piggin of York. Turn left down the road (White Kirkley sign missing), cross the bridge over Bollihope Beck and up to the hamlet of White Kirkley.

Continue, fairly steeply up the lane and follow in the footsteps of the shepherds, miners and quarrymen on this old highway. This gated lane becomes unenclosed, as it gradually climbs uphill for over a mile, with wonderful views of Weardale. As you pass Allotment House, a tall stone barn, the lane deteriorates into a rutted track and leads you out through a gate onto Pikestone Fell. Turn left along a broad track for a bracing walk on the moor edge, perched high above Weardale with extensive views. You will pass a clump of trees known locally as The Elephant Trees.

Continue eastwards, the stone wall on your left and follow the rutted track for 1½ miles, giving views southwards of the old lead mine spoil heaps on Pikestone Fell.

As you pass the entrance to Harthope, continue eastwards through an open gateway into an enclosed track and follow this for a mile to reach the Hamsterley/Wolsingham Road. Turn left down the steep road known as Wear Bank and admire the aeriel views of Wolsingham. Follow this road for 1½ miles back to Wolsingham.

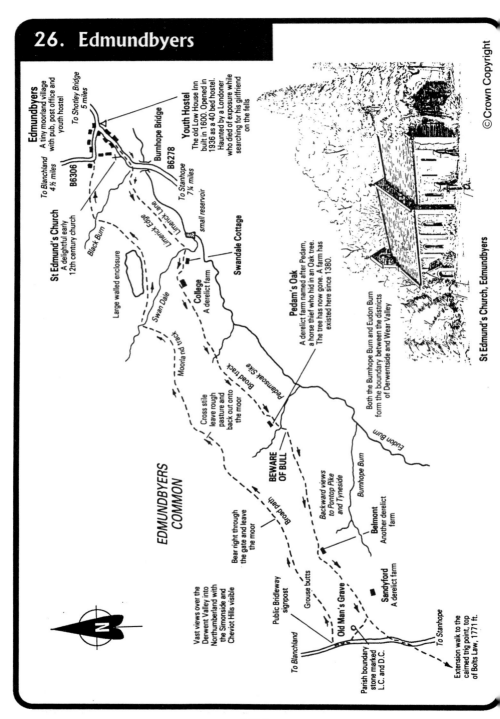

© Crown Copyright

Edmundbyers
A tiny moorland village with pub, post office and youth hostel

To Shotley Bridge 5 miles

Youth Hostel
The old Low House Inn built in 1600. Opened in 1936 as a 40 bed hostel. Haunted by a Londoner who died of exposure while searching for his girlfriend on the fells

Burnhope Bridge

B6278

To Blanchland 4½ miles

B6306

St Edmund's Church
A delightful early 12th century church

To Stanhope 7¼ miles

Black Burn

Limerick Lane

Limerick Edge

small reservoir

Swandale Cottage

Large walled enclosure

Swan Dale

College
A derelict farm

Pedam's Oak
A derelict farm named after Pedam, a horse thief who hid in an Oak tree. The tree has now gone. A farm has existed here since 1380.

Moorla rd track

Broad track

Pedemsoak Sike

Both the Burnhope Burn and Eudon Burn form the boundary between the districts of Derwentside and Wear Valley

Cross stile leave rough pasture and back out onto the moor

Eudon Burn

BEWARE OF BULL

Backward views to Pontop Pike and Tyneside

Burnhope Burn

Belmont
Another derelict farm

EDMUNDBYERS COMMON

Bear right through the gate and leave the moor

Broad path

Public Bridleway signpost

Grouse butts

Vast views over the Derwent Valley into Northumberland with the Simonside and Cheviot Hills visible

Old Man's Grave

Sandyford
A derelict farm

To Blanchland

Parish boundary stone marked L.C. and D.C.

To Stanhope

Extension walk to the cairned trig point, top of Bolts Law, 1771 ft.

N

St Edmund's Church, Edmundbyers

26. Edmundbyers

Route: *Edmundbyers — College — Pedam's Oak — Belmont — Edmundbyers Common — Edmundbyers.*
Distance: *About 9 miles (14.5km). Moderate. Allow 4/5 hours*
O.S. Maps: *Landranger Sheet 87; Pathfinder Sheets NZ05/15; 571 (NZ04/14); NY84/94.*
Public Transport: *Laws Travel 773, OK Travel 869. Check timetables.*
Parking: *Limited roadside parking in Edmundbyers.*
Refreshments: *The Punch Bowl, Edmundbyers. None on route.*
Note: *Very exposed in bad weather.*

This moorland walk explores the unknown Burnhope Burn, a peaceful Pennine valley in a quiet corner of north-west Durham. It is one of England's last areas of wild country and offers an escape for those who enjoy the peace and solitude of the bleak moorlands, with magnificent views.

Start from Edmundbyers and leave this moorland village by walking west down the B6278 Stanhope road. Pop in to the delightful early twelfth century church of St Edmund. Where the road bends by the wooden seat, turn right into the unsignposted Limerick Lane, which used to be the ancient highway to Allenheads.

Follow this unsurfaced, gated lane westwards and after a mile, cross the small stream at Swandale Foot and ascend the stony track for a fairly stiff climb, the only real climb on the walk. At the top, turn left by the derelict farm called College, the first of three derelict farmhouses on the outward route.

Head west along the gated broad bridleway track with detailed direction not needed. Take a backward view down the bleak Burnhope Burn and see the television transmitting mast of Pontop Pike, plus the distant tall tower blocks of Tyneside.

A mile further on, as you approach the next farm, there are three metal gates. Take the left one and pass in front of Pedam's Oak, where a farm has existed since 1380.

This derelict farm is named after Pedam, a horse thief who hid in a decayed oak tree. Go through a couple of farm gates (re-close), cross Pedamsoak Sike and ascend the track through a metal gate, where you might encounter a bull among the grazing cattle.

Carry on for a mile to the final abandoned farm called Belmont and turn right and pass the farm on your left. Cross the stile (one of three on the entire walk) by the gate and turn left along the rough-rutted farm track that merges by the moor wall for a short way on your left.

On the horizon the view includes the twin chimney tops of the bygone lead mining industry and the trig point top of Bolts Law (1,773 ft), a fine extension walk for another day.

When you reach a facing padlocked gate, pass this on your left and bear right, up the track to straddle a stile by a facing gate, noting the rounded stone about two feet high resembling a gravestone marked L.C. and D.C. — this is a parish boundary stone erected under the Commons Enclosure Act of 1800. This particular spot is marked on the O.S. map as Old Man's Grave. I wonder why?

Go straight on to reach the Stanhope — Blanchland road and turn up this for glorious views over the Derwent Valley into Northumberland to the Simonside and Cheviot Hills. At the public bridleway signpost, turn right for the return route which is over Edmundbyers Common.

At first the moor is pathless, but then you pick up a path which becomes a track, as you head eastwards down to a line of grouse butts to go through a gate in the facing wire fence. Stride out along a mile of moorland track which slants down to a gate in the boundary fence. Go through this and turn left along the rough pasture, where at its eastern end, negotiate the stile over the barbed wire fence for a return to the moor. The view eastwards now includes Edmundbyers Village.

Carry on by following the moor path for another mile to cross the stream over Swandale, where the track contours right above Limerick Edge to pass a large walled enclosure on your left. Keep on the track which goes downhill to ford the Black Burn. Follow the gated bridle track which brings you out on the Blanchland road and go downhill to end this splendid walk back in Edmundbyers.

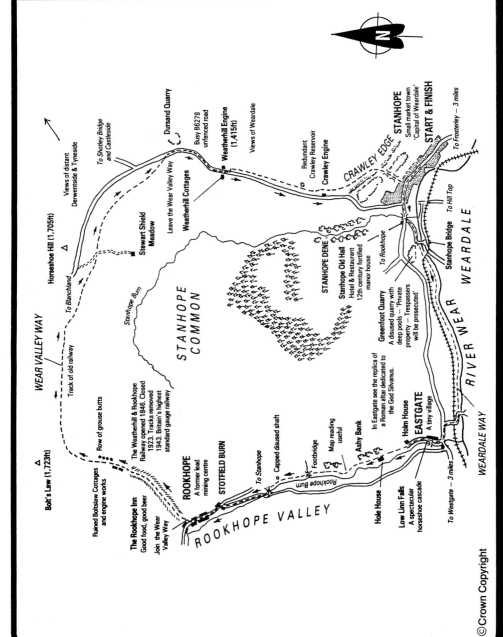

STANHOPE
Small market town
'Capital of Weardale'
START & FINISH

To Frosterley — 3 miles

CRAWLEY EDGE

Dursand Quarry

To Shotley Bridge
and Castleside

Busy B6278
unfenced road

Weatherhill Engine
(1,415ft)

Views of Weardale

Redundant
Crawley Reservoir

Crawley Engine

Views of distant
Derwentside & Tyneside

Leave the Wear Valley Way

Weatherhill Cottages

Horseshoe Hill (1,705ft)

Stewart Shield
Meadow

To Blanchland

WEAR VALLEY WAY

Stanhope Burn

STANHOPE
COMMON

STANHOPE DENE

Stanhope Old Hall
Hotel & Restaurant
12th century fortified
manor house

To Rookhope

Stanhope Bridge

To Hill Top

WEARDALE

RIVER WEAR

Greenfoot Quarry
A disused quarry with
deep pools — Private
property — Trespassers
will be prosecuted'

Track of old railway

Bolt's Law (1,723ft)

Ruined Boltslaw Cottages
and engine works

Row of grouse butts

The Weatherhill & Rookhope
Railway opened 1846. Closed
1923. Tracks removed
1943. Britain's highest
standard gauge railway

ROOKHOPE
A former lead
mining centre

The Rookhope Inn
Good food, good beer

Join the Wear
Valley Way

STOTFIELD BURN

To Stanhope

Capped disused shaft

Footbridge

Map reading
useful

Ashy Bank

In Eastgate see the replica of
a Roman altar dedicated to
the God Silvanus.

Holm House

EASTGATE
A tiny village

Rookhope Burn

Hole House

Low Linn Falls
A spectacular
horseshoe cascade

To Westgate — 3 miles

WEARDALE WAY

ROOKHOPE VALLEY

27. Stanhope

Route: *Stanhope — Eastgate — Rookhope — Boltslaw Incline — Crawley Incline — Stanhope.*
Distance: *Over 13 miles (20km). Clockwise circuit. Moderate/strenuous. Meadow and moorland. Allow 7½ hours.*
O.S. Maps: *Landranger Sheets 92 and 87.*
Public Transport: *Buses — Weardale Services 101, Bishop Auckland to Stanhope; trains — The Heritage Line, which is extended from Bishop Auckland to Stanhope for summer Sundays.*
Refreshments: *Pubs, hotels and cafes in Stanhope; Cross Keys, Eastgate; The Rookhope Inn, Rookhope.*
Warning: *Do not explore the old mine shafts — they are dangerous and unsafe. Keep out of the old quarries with deep pools.*
Note: *Do not attempt in doubtful weather.*

Early May is the best time for this meadow and moorland walk in Weardale, especially if you want to see wild flowers and wide expansive views.

The first part is a splendid walk from Stanhope to Eastgate on low level paths along the River Wear, using the Weardale Way, which also explores the remote Rookhope Valley. The second part encounters the Wear Valley Way for a bracing upland walk, via old railway inclines with magnificent views.

Leave Stanhope by walking west along the A689 and opposite Stanhope Hall, turn left down the B6278 by Horn Hall Hospital and follow the road to Stanhope Bridge. Do not cross the bridge, but turn right along the gated track (path sign missing) and pass the disused Greenfoot Quarry.

Beyond the quarry, fork left and cross a couple of stiles on either side of the mineral railway line. Turn right along the meadow, keep by the electric fence and walk westwards for 2½ miles through some fine riverside scenery, dotted with golden gorse bushes. Detailed direction is not necessary but watch for a concealed corner stile by the fenced railway, beyond the riverside cottage.

Upstream, go through a wooden gate into Hag Bridge Caravan Park (check map) and where the track goes through a gateway, turn left along the path by the wall and exit over a difficult stile at the end of Hag Bank Bridge. Turn right up the road, noting the old Eastgate Station to reach the A689.

Turn left and enter Eastgate, a tiny village which once marked the boundary of the Bishop of Durham's deer park. A Roman altar, dedicated to the God Silvanus and dating back to AD 238-244, was found in the Rookhope Burn on November 15, 1869. Beside the phone box, see the replica of the altar, unveiled a hundred years later, on the exact date of its discovery.

From Eastgate, walk north up the lane by the Cuthbert Bainbridge Memorial Chapel (1891) and beyond All Saints' Church, turn left by Rose Cottage and right behind another cottage for an interesting diversion to see Low Linn Falls, a hidden horseshoe cascade. The waterfalls are well worth a visit.

Return and go up the walled lane: it is a steep pull up, with great views of the Rookhope Valley and its waterfalls. Head northwards, pass Holme House on your right, where the lane deteriorates into a track and when you reach Hole House, do not go through the gate marked "No Road", but take the gate tied with twine on your right.

Go up Ashy Bank for a woodland walk carpeted with wild flowers, mainly primroses and bluebells. At the top, go through a gate and turn left for a level walk high above the wooded Rookhope Burn. Keep by the fence at first and gradually fork left downhill on a track that leads to the Rookhope Burn. Turn right in front of some fenced gateposts and head north for an up-and-down valley walk.

Constantly check the map as you climb above the wooded valley and where it levels out, see the patches of primroses among the rocky outcrops. Here, if you are quiet, you might be lucky to see a deer. Back down the burn and over a white-painted footbridge, cross a boggy section churned up by cattle and keep on the lower path by the burn. You will pass roofless buildings and fenced old shafts, a reminder of the bygone lead mining industry.

Once out of the wood, pass a capped disused shaft and cross a footbridge over Rookhope Burn to reach the Rookhope — Eastgate road. Turn right along the road for a mile to reach the moorland village of Rookhope, a former lead mining centre. This is your last opportunity for buying refreshments, so call in at The Rookhope Inn, where Alex Lee welcomes walkers.

Opposite Rookhope Post Office, turn right up the unsurfaced track (footpath signposted) with the street sign "Leading to Hylton Terrace" and follow the Wear Valley Way up past a group of garages. As you climb, look back over the roof tops of Rookhope and see the extent of this remote valley.

Where the track splits, fork left and go through a metal gate out onto the open moorland at the foot of the old railway incline. Head straight up the Boltslaw Incline for a steady, but stiff climb up to the old ruins at Bolts Law engine works. This sec-

(Continued on page 108)

107

(Continued from page 107)

tion was the highest standard-gauge railway line ever built in the United Kingdom. From the engine works, stay on the disused line, all the way round for a further four miles until you reach the B6278.

This high level route skirts Stanhope Common south of Bolts Law and offers superb views of wild Weardale. Turn right along the unfenced B6278 for a mile to the whitewashed Weatherhill Cottages and cross the road to Weatherhill Engine. Head southwards down the disused Stanhope and Tyne Valley Railway, using the Crawleyside Incline for 1½ miles, noting the old marker stones inscribed with "S. & D.R.".

Leave the walkway, as you approach a partially-renovated house (site of the Crawley Engine), turn left along a track and once through the gate posts, turn right by the garden wall of the same house. Follow the track and veer left, eastwards along Crawley Edge. Keep on this broad path until it forks right down the edge, aiming for a couple of kissing gates, and bears left for a stile that directs you over a couple of girder bridges over the extensive Ashes Quarry.

Continue downhill into an enclosed path that leads you into Stanhope. Turn left along Chapel Street and return to Stanhope Market Place.

109

110

The Wear between Wolsingham and Frosterley (Walk 25, p102).

Along the banks of Gunnerside Gill (Walk 8, p38).

FASHION FACTORY SHOP

Great Choice — Great Value
NEW DELIVERIES EVERY DAY

CLOTHES FOR ALL SEASONS

- Wedding Outfits
- Mix 'n Match Separates
- Leisurewear for Men
- A Selection of Childrenswear

plus many more exciting new fashions

Over 6,000 high quality items give you the best fashion choice in the North East

SATURDAY, MONDAY, TUESDAY, WEDNESDAY, FRIDAY
10 a.m. to 5 p.m.
THURSDAY
10 a.m. to 6.30 p.m.

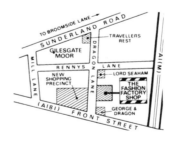

DRAGON LANE, DRAGONVILLE IND. ESTATE
GILESGATE MOOR, DURHAM CITY
Telephone (091) 3843212

50-070

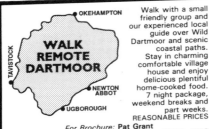

28. Sunderland Bridge

Route: Sunderland Bridge — Croxdale Hall — Croxdale Wood House — High Butterby Farm — Shincliffe — Strawberry Lane — High Croxdale Farm — Croxdale Hall — Sunderland Bridge.
Distance: Over 7 miles (11 km). Allow 3½ hours. Fairly easy to moderate. Parkland, woodland, riverside and field paths with some unavoidable road walking.
O.S. Maps: Landranger Sheets 93 and 88; Pathfinder Sheets NZ 23/33 and NZ 24/34
Parking: Sunderland Bridge (the old road bridge over the River Wear) Croxdale, off A167 (GR 265377).
Public Transport: United 6, 722, 723. OK Travel 724 to Sunderland Bridge. Check timetables.
Refreshments: The Seven Stars, Shincliffe.
Note: Keep to the bridle road through Croxdale Estate. Observe the notices "Croxdale Wood — Private — Keep Out"; "These woods are private — please keep out" — Croxdale Estate. Useful to carry both the O.S. Pathfinder Maps. Dogs must be on lead at all times. Stout footwear recommended, woodland paths very slippery and muddy after wet weather.

Discover the delights of the Durham countryside with a seven-mile saunter between Sunderland Bridge and Shincliffe, south of Durham City.

The outward route follows part of the Weardale Way and uses parkland, woodland and riverside paths. The return is along Strawberry Lane, a lesser known drovers route that once served Ferryhill and Durham City.

Start from the parking end of old Sunderland Bridge and go through the entrance gates into Croxdale Estate. Follow the carriageway under the A167 road and keep to the bridle road along an avenue of sycamore trees, where a number of notices marked "Private — Keep Off" relate to the delightful parkland.

Once over a cattle grid, cross the stone bridge over Croxdale Beck and uphill, look for a short cut — three sets of separate steps (18 in all) on your right. Alternatively, you can follow the drive round and up past the elegant Croxdale Hall — the seat of the Salvin family and still the home of this well-known county family. The hall was built about 1760 by General Salvin and is not open to public view.

Turn left and pass the disused medieval church (private), where directly ahead you will see the impressive, huge stone barn called locally 'The Hay Shed', now redundant and a reminder of by-gone days.

Between the church and barn, turn left then right up the narrow surfaced lane with views of Burn Hall and Brandon. This pleasant lane hugs Croxdale Wood with a couple of notices telling you to keep out of this private wood.

After 880 yards, pass Croxdale Wood House and turn right by Woodhouse Cottage, where the lane becomes an unsurfaced farm track by Butterby Wood. There are fine views with Thrislington Works and Kirk Merrington visible.

A half-mile further on pass the white-washed High Butterby Farm on your left and turn right, where in yards, a yellow way-marked post — public footpath — directs you left into Shincliffe Wood, a

delightful woodland maintained by the Dean and Chapter of Durham Cathedral. You will encounter some high vegetation at first, then go down the steps into a dark, deep woodland by a wire fence for a fairly steep descent, downwards to the banks of the River Wear.

Turn right downstream and follow the wooded riverside path via a series of steps. When the river path ends, turn right away from the river by the tree with the notice "Durham AC Private Fishing" fixed to it and follow the path for 880 yards within the woodland edge to pass Shincliffe Hall, a fine brick-built house used by Durham University Graduate Society.

Turn up Hall Lane for 880 yards to Shincliffe Village. As you walk along this single surfaced lane you will see the central tower of Durham cathedral peeping out above Houghall Woods.

When you reach the pretty village of Shincliffe turn right along the tree-lined main street, with its hidden parish church and pass The Seven Stars which serves hot and cold meals, to reach the A177 road. Turn right along this main road, use the footways for 880 yards and uphill at the sign High Shincliffe (bypass road), cross this busy road with extreme care to the tarmac lane opposite called Strawberry Lane, a drovers route once used by peasants and farmers between Ferryhill and Durham City.

Follow this quiet lane southwards and where it bends right, walk forward along the unsignposted, short track to cross a stile by an open gap. Turn left along the field edge, then right in front of a rusty gate and follow the path by the hedge within the same field. At the end of this field, go through the gap into an enclosed hedgerowed path and as you progress southwards, you will see the old grandstand of Shincliffe racecourse (private — keep out), which is now used as a hay barn.

(Continued on page 125)

123

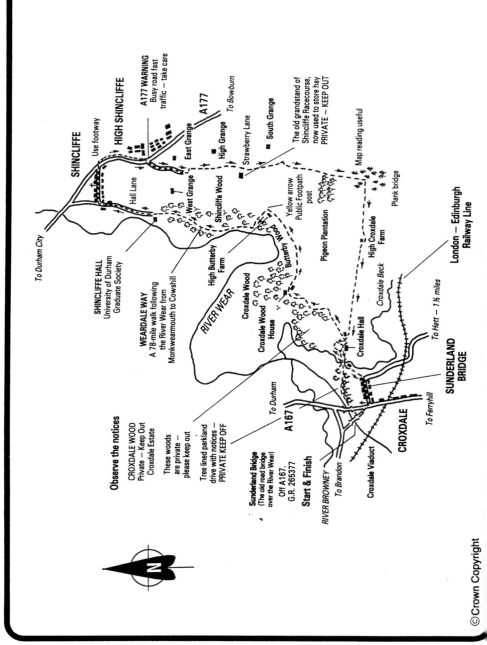

SHINCLIFFE

Use footway

HIGH SHINCLIFFE

A177 WARNING
Busy road fast
traffic — take care

A177

To Bowburn

East Grange

High Grange

South Grange

Strawberry Lane

The old grandstand of
Shincliffe Racecourse,
now used to store hay
PRIVATE — KEEP OUT

Map reading useful

Hall Lane

West Grange

Shincliffe Wood

Yellow arrow
Public Footpath
post

Plank bridge

To Durham City

SHINCLIFFE HALL
University of Durham
Graduate Society

WEARDALE WAY
A 78-mile walk following
the River Wear from
Monkwearmouth to Cowshill

High Butterby
Farm

RIVER WEAR

Butterby Wood

Pigeon Plantation

High Croxdale
Farm

Croxdale Beck

London — Edinburgh
Railway Line

Croxdale Wood

Croxdale Wood
House

Croxdale Hall

To Hett — 1½ miles

Observe the notices

CROXDALE WOOD
Private — Keep Out
Croxdale Estate

These woods
are private —
please keep out

Tree lined parkland
drive with notices —
PRIVATE KEEP OFF

To Durham

A167

SUNDERLAND
BRIDGE

Sunderland Bridge
(The old road bridge
over the River Wear)
Off A167.
G.R. 265377
Start & Finish

RIVER BROWNEY

To Brandon

Croxdale Viaduct

CROXDALE

To Ferryhill

N

(Continued from page 123)

Continue straight on along a stony track and once through a squeeze gap, enter an enclosed lane and exit through a stile. Cross the farm road, carry straight on along a broad farm road and cross a stile by a gate. Further on, go through a gate by Pigeon Plantation and follow the faint path by the drainage ditch and broom bushes. At the end of the field, cross a stile by a gate and follow the path through a narrow belt of young fir trees. So far along (check O.S. map), when you reach a path traversing left and right, turn right along this, cross a plank bridge and go through the gap in the fence by the gate.

Follow the field edge, cross a stile by a gate and follow the enclosed path to join a track that leads you round the renovated, white-washed High Croxdale Farm. Now follow the broad track for 880 yards down to Croxdale Hall. Return by the outward route or after crossing the bridge over Croxdale Beck, bear left past The Mill for a steep climb up to the pretty village of Sunderland Bridge.

Return to old road bridge over the River Wear or Sunderland Bridge.

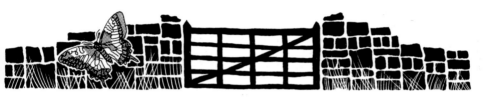

125

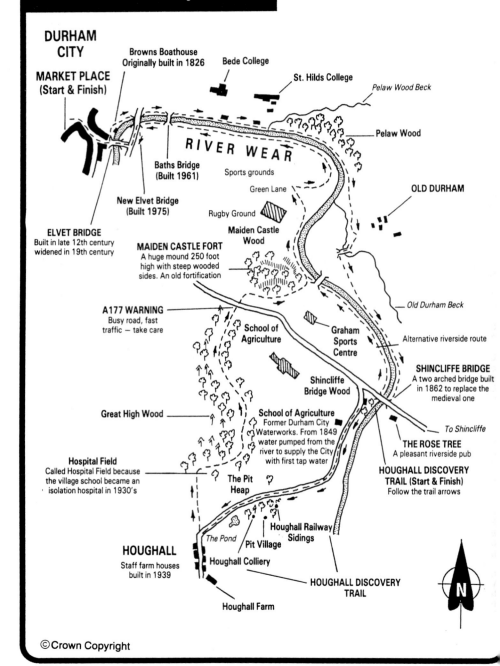

DURHAM CITY

MARKET PLACE
(Start & Finish)

Browns Boathouse
Originally built in 1826

Bede College

St. Hilds College

Pelaw Wood Beck

RIVER WEAR

Pelaw Wood

Baths Bridge
(Built 1961)

Sports grounds

Green Lane

OLD DURHAM

New Elvet Bridge
(Built 1975)

Rugby Ground

ELVET BRIDGE
Built in late 12th century
widened in 19th century

Maiden Castle
Wood

MAIDEN CASTLE FORT
A huge mound 250 foot
high with steep wooded
sides. An old fortification

Old Durham Beck

A177 WARNING
Busy road, fast
traffic — take care

School of
Agriculture

Graham
Sports
Centre

Alternative riverside route

SHINCLIFFE BRIDGE
A two arched bridge built
in 1862 to replace the
medieval one

Shincliffe
Bridge Wood

Great High Wood

School of Agriculture
Former Durham City
Waterworks. From 1849
water pumped from the
river to supply the City
with first tap water

To Shincliffe

THE ROSE TREE
A pleasant riverside pub

Hospital Field
Called Hospital Field because
the village school became an
isolation hospital in 1930's

The Pit
Heap

**HOUGHALL DISCOVERY
TRAIL (Start & Finish)**
Follow the trail arrows

Houghall Railway
Sidings

The Pond / Pit Village

HOUGHALL
Staff farm houses
built in 1939

Houghall Colliery

**HOUGHALL DISCOVERY
TRAIL**

Houghall Farm

N

29. Durham City

Route: Durham City — Elvet Bridge — Pelaw Wood — Shincliffe Bridge — Houghall — Great High Wood — Maiden Castle Wood — Green Lane — Baths Bridge — Durham City.
Distance: Over 4½ miles. Allow 2½/3 hours. Riverside, field and woodland paths plus lanes.
O.S. Maps: Landranger Sheet 88;Pathfinder Sheet NZ24/34.
Public Transport: Regular bus and train services to Durham City.
Parking: City car parks, Cathedral, Milburngate, Riverside Ice Rink and Framwellgate. All pay car parks.
Refreshments: Plenty of hotels, cafes and pubs in Durham City. The Rose Tree, Shincliffe.

We are lucky to have a delightful riverside ramble on Durham's doorstep. This short stroll, on both sides of the River Wear, is a gem of a walk with an invitation to follow part of the Houghall Discovery Trail, a two-mile walk through history, a mile or so south of Durham City. It is an enjoyable experience and certainly well worth the diversion.

Leave Durham City Market Place by Fleshergate and turn left down Elvet to the city end of Elvet Bridge. By Bramwell's the opticians, go down Elvet Steps to the riverside towpath below, noting the nine arched ancient Elvet Bridge. Turn left, follow the towpath behind Brown's Boathouse and proceed by the River Wear to go under New Elvet Bridge. Onwards, pass Baths Bridge built in 1962 to replace an iron footbridge. Use this footbridge on the return route.

Look back for one of the best scenic sights in Europe — the medieval city of Durham dominated by its Cathedral and Castle. Follow the riverside by the renowned Regatta Course, with the College of St Hild and St Bede up to your left and the Old Racecourse across the river.

At the end of the towpath, enter Pelaw Wood and follow the path along the wooded riverside. Out of the wood, ignore the path up to your left and proceed straight on, diagonally left across a rough pasture, to join a track that swings left by the dismantled railway embankment (abandoned 1956). Turn right through the demolished railway bridge, cross a stile and over another stile, cross the metal footbridge over Old Durham Beck. Turn left and aim between the football fields for the unusual suspension bridge. Do not cross the bridge, but turn left along the field edge to join the embanked riverside path and along a cart track to come out on to the A177, opposite The Rose Tree Inn, a pleasant riverside pub.

From the pub, turn left along the A177 and cross the twin-arched Shincliffe Bridge over the River Wear and 30 yards beyond, take the unsignposted lane on your left. At the car park on your left, you have the opportunity to join the Houghall Discovery Trail officially opened in October, 1988. This two-mile trail is well worth following. Enter

the small Shincliffe Bridge Wood and follow the path to the first of nine boards, which explain and illustrate the surrounding landscape changes.

Rejoin the lane and the Houghall Farm Horticultural Unit on your right is the old waterworks which supplied Durham with its first tap water. Continue along the lane, follow the Discovery Trail arrows and the woodland on your right is a pit heap, camouflaged by trees planted in the 1920s by Durham County Council and thought to be the first ever reclamation of an industrial eyesore.

Further on, the trail leads through a handgate on your left into a woodland with an interesting trio — Houghall Railway Sidings and the remains of an abandoned colliery and pit village, where a chapel and school existed. Return to the lane, turn left and next on the trail is a recently excavated pond, which was once a depressing swamp.

On reaching the staff houses of Houghall, my route misses out a couple of the trail's interesting information boards, but encounters the return route of the trail. Turn right and follow the yellow waymark arrows along the holly-hedgerowed lane, cross the step board stile by a gate and hug the holly hedge on your left. At the top of the field there is another information board telling you that this field is called Hospital Field because the village school became an isolation hospital.

Cross the corner stile into Great High Wood and turn right along the path within the woodland edge. Keep on this path, giving good views across the fertile flood plain to the Durham College of Agriculture and Horticulture. Cross the busy A177 and enter Maiden Castle Wood. Follow the path round the base of the wooded prehistoric site of Maiden Castle, a 250ft mound. It has been suggested that it was an old fortification. Do not be tempted to cross the suspension bridge, but turn left and join the riverside path which takes you past the old demolished railway bridge and leads into Green Lane.

Turn right along the surfaced lane to come out by Durham Amateur Rowing Club and follow the paved path alongside the River Wear to cross Baths Bridge and return by the outward route to complete a delightful scenic amble.

HIGH WARDEN HILL (593 feet above sea level)
Known locally as "Watch Hill" or "Camp Hill."
A trig point summit occupied by a large
Iron Age Fort. Excellent views of Tynedale
and the North and South Tyne Valleys

RIVER NORTH TYNE

WARDEN
A hidden hamlet, with St Michael
and All Angels Church Consecrated in
AD 704. Famous for its Saxon tower

**MEETING OF THE WATERS
OR WATERSMEET**
Where the North and South Tyne
meet or where the Tyne splits

Warden Bridge
Stone road bridge, replaced an 1826 suspension
bridge in 1903. See Toll Bridge Cottage, a former
toll house

**BEWARE OF
THE BULL**

**HIGH
WARDEN**

**Private Walk
Wood**

BRIDGE END

To Hexham

West Boat

To A69

Laverick Plantation

Alternative route

Please shut
the gate — fasten
chain

**Warden Methodist
Chapel T.M. 1896**

The Boatside Inn
Built in 1857. (British Relais Routiers
Recommended). Restaurant-Bar meals

FOURSTONES VILLAGE
It derives its name from four
Roman altar stones used to mark
the original boundries of the
medieval village

Start & Finish

*To Newbrough
— 1 mile*

To Carlisle

TYNE VALLEY LINE

RIVER SOUTH TYNE

Fourstones Paper Mill
The mill was established in 1763
by Rev. Peter Rumney. It is one of
the oldest paper mills in the country

Hardhaugh Cottages
Inscription above end
cottage — "This school
was built by subscription
in 1820"

Riverside Cottage
"This is private land over
which there is a public right
of way along the top of the
river bank only — Please keep
to the footpath"

THE RAILWAY INN
'Doon the bank'

N

30. Fourstones

Route: Fourstones — Bridge End — Warden — High Warden — Warden Hill — Fourstones.
Distance: Over 4 miles (6.5km). Fairly easy. Allow 2½ to 3 hours.
O.S. Maps: Landranger Sheet 87; Pathfinder Sheet NY86/96.
Parking: Very limited road side parking in Fourstones village 4 miles west of Hexham.
Public Transport: Tyne Valley Coaches, Hexham to Newbrough. Daily Monday to Saturday but check timetables.
Refreshments: The Railway Inn, Fourstones; The Boatside Inn, Bridge End.
Note: Expect plenty of mud, stout footwear needed.

Fourstones, a tiny Tynedale village, four miles west of Hexham, is the perfect starting place for a riverside stroll along the South Tyne Valley to the Watersmeet or Meeting of the Waters, where the North and South Tyne join and the Tyne splits.

The walk calls in at the hidden hamlet of Warden, with its lovely church boasting the oldest Saxon tower in Northumberland. The return via High Warden offers an interesting diversion up to Warden Hill, giving the best views of Tynedale.

Leave Fourstones opposite St Aidan's Church and go "Doon The Bank" to the Railway Inn. Cross the Tyne Valley Railway with care and observe the warning signs "Stop, Look, Listen — Beware of Trains". At Riverside Cottage a notice states "This is private land over which there is a public right of way along the top of the river bank only. Please keep to the footpath." As requested, turn left in front of this beautifully-built stone cottage and keep to the footpath.

You have now joined the River South Tyne and follow this riverside path eastwards by the broom bushes downstream for 880 yards. Where the path splits, check the O.S. Map and look out for a white kissing gate wedged by the wall and barbed wire fence. Leave the river, go through the gate and follow the path along the rough pasture with high broom bushes for a watery walk. Exit through a corner gate and rejoin the riverside path which is very muddy after wet weather.

Stroll downstream for 880 yards to come out by Fourstones Paper Mill. Turn right and pass the mill, established by the Rev Peter Rumney and William Charnley in 1763. It is one of the country's oldest paper mills.

Follow the road, pass Hardhaugh Cottages, noting the inscription above the end cottage which reads "This school was built by subscription in 1820". Further on, pass Warden Methodist Chapel 1896) to reach Bridge End, where the Boatside Inn is an excellent pub for bar meals.

A nearby Public Footpath sign "Meeting of the Waters" directs you along the riverside path for a mere and back walk of half-a-mile each way to the meeting of the Waters, where the North and South Tyne join. It is worth the walk, just to say you have been the Watersmeet.

By the Boatside Inn, turn left along the road to the hidden hamlet of Warden, where people have been worshipping at Warden Church since it was founded by St Wilfrid in AD 704. This lovely church is well worth a visit.

From Warden, turn right up the road for 880 yards with excellent views east over the North Tyne to the little village of Acomb towards Hexham.

At the Public Bridleway signpost "Fourstones 1½", turn left, cross the cattle grid and follow the main driveway which curves left uphill to the estate cottages of High Warden. Bear right, walk straight on by the row of cottages, now holiday homes, past Staindale Cottage on your left and follow the muddy cart track into the edge of Private Walk Wood.

Turn right up the edge of the wood and at the top, go through a white metal gate, where you join a broad cart track. Follow this to the top of the field, go through a wooden gate and turn immediately left by a clump of trees and along the field edge and out through another wooden gate. Aim half right, diagonally up the next pasture and straddle the corner wall with wooden supports either side.

From here there is an interesting diversion, so turn right up by the wall edge to the trig point top of High Warden Hill (593ft), with an ancient earthwork on its summit. No wonder it's known locally as "Watch Hill" or "Camp Hill" because of its look-out position. You can see both the North and South Tyne Valleys plus a bird's eye view of Tynedale and all Hexhamshire.

Retrace your steps and look out for the bull among the grazing cattle. Keep by the bottom wall and turn left through a gate into Laverick Plantation. Go down the slanting path through the wood and out onto a broad bridle track that has come up from Quality Cottages. Turn up this track with the plantation on your right, where at the top, a gap in the trees gives a glimpse of Chollerford in the North Tyne Valley.

The track curves round to the left with a small cottage on your right and leads you through a wooden gate and down the sloping field edge. Turn left through a way-marked red metal gate (please fasten chain) and turn right down the gated cart track and through the farmyard for a return to the village of Fourstones to end a very satisfying walk.

130

SERVICE AVAILABLE DURING MOST NORTH COUNTRY WALKS

50-070

134

135

140

COUNTRYSIDE EVENTS in CLEVELAND

COUNTRYSIDE EVENTS IN CLEVELAND

It's all happening out there in Cleveland's Countryside Guided Walks, Conservation Activity Days, Cross Country Skiing, Bird Watches, Countryside Craft Days, Fun Runs and lots of fun and games for all the family.

Events are organised by Cleveland County Council's Countryside Wardens and take place in these four main areas.

The River Tees Valley — from Yarm to Teesmouth.
Billingham Beck Valley and Ecology Park — alongside the A19 between Norton and Billingham.
Castle Eden Walkway Country Park — beside the A177 at Thorpe Thewles.
Lazenby Bank — signposted off the A174 near Lazenby Village and Wilton ICI.

For further information and events leaflets contact:
Project Officer: Carol Raper
Tel. (0642) 248155 ext. 2427

J. D. S. Gillis, Director, Department of Economic Development and Planning, Cleveland County Council, Gurney House, Gurney Street, Middlesbrough, Cleveland. TS1 1QT.   50 070

Cleveland County Council
DEPARTMENT OF ECONOMIC DEVELOPMENT & PLANNING

141

Other walks

Here is a selection of some of my walks that have appeared in the weekly series with The Northern Echo, but are not included in this volume.

North York Moors/Heritage Coast:
- Saltburn — Skinningrove — Boulby — Staithes (8 miles);
- Egton Bridge — Briggswath — Ruswarp — Whitby (8 miles);
- Danby Lodge — Ainthorpe — Danby Rigg, Danby Lodge (4 miles);
- Hutton-le-Hole — Ana Cross — Lastingham — Hutton-le-Hole (9 miles);
- Clay Bank — Urra Moor — Chop Gate — Cold Moor — Clay Bank (8 miles);
- The Cleveland Street, Guisborough to Loftus (9 miles);
- Great Ayton — Roseberry Topping — Capt. Cook's Momument — Great Ayton (7 miles);
- Swainby — Beacon Hill — Osmotherley — Sheepwash — Swainby (9 miles);
- Newgate Bank — Sun Inn — Roppa Edge — Newgate Bank (9 miles);

Yorkshire Dales:
- The Elgar Way, Settle — Giggleswick — Stainforth — Settle (13 miles);
- Buckden — Starbotton — Bucken Pike — Cray — Buckden (10 miles);
- Swineside — Bradley — Horsehouse — Swineside (10 miles);
- Hawes — Hardraw Force — High Shaw — Sedbusk — Hawes (7 miles);
- Askrigg — Woodall — Carperby — Disher Force — Askrigg (9 miles);
- Richmond — Easby — Skeeby — Gilling West — Richmond (9 miles);
- Richmond — Hudswell Woods — Hudswell — Richmond (5 miles);
- Reeth — Blades — Gunnerside — Low Whita — Reeth (13 miles);

Masham/Ripon/Easingwold Area:
- Grewelthorpe — Mickley — West Tanfield — Mickley — Grewelthorpe (5/10 miles);
- Kirby Malzeard — Galphay — Winksley — High Grantley — Laverton — Kirby Malzeard (11 miles);
- Easingwold — Husthwaite — Coxwold — Oulston — Easingwold (10 miles);

Durham Dales (Teesdale)
- Cotherstone — Hury Reservoir — Butter Stone — Cotherstone (7 miles);
- Middleton in Teesdale — Coldberry Mine — Skears Quarry — Middleton in Teesdale (7 miles);
- Middleton in Teesdale — Bowlees — High Force — Low Force — Middleton in Teesdale (10 miles);

Wear Valley/Central Durham
- Bishop Auckland — Escomb — Etherley Moor — Bishop Auckland (4 miles);
- Sunderland Bridge — Brandon/Bishop Rail Walk — Page Bank — Spennymoor — Sunderland Bridge (11 miles);

Tynedale/Allendale/Northumberland
- Low Prudhoe — Ovingham — Whittle Dene — Horsley — Low Prudhoe (5 miles);
- Wylam — Clara Vale — Crawcrook — Greenside — Coalburns — Wylam (10 miles);
- Allendale Town — Catton — Catton Beacon — Allenmill Bridge — Allendale Town (7 miles);
- Belsay — Bolam — Shaftoe Craggs — West Tofthill — Belsay (10 miles);

Your enjoyment of all the walks in this book and in the weekly series in The Northern Echo can be further enhanced if you purchase some of the excellent range of cards and leaflets available in villages and churches, including the Local History Cards series by Gatehouse Prints.

Bibliography

These guide books should provide interesting background reading for walkers:

Earnshaw, Alan — The Wear Valley Way (Discovery Guides 1983)
Emett, Charlie — Walking Northern Railways Vol 1, East (Cicerone Press 1988)
Hannon, Paul — Walks in Swaledale (Hillside Publications 1987)
Hannon, Paul — Walks in Wharfedale (Hillside Publications 1985)
Hannon, Paul — Walks in Wensleydale (Hillside Publications 1987)
Hannon, Paul — Walks on the North York Moors: Western, Southern, Northern (Hillside Publications 1988)
North York Moors National Park — Family Walks Around Sutton Bank (North York Moors National Park 1988)
Piggin, Ken — Weardale Way (Dalesman 1984)
Ramblers' Association — Walking in the Northern Dales (Dalesman 1977)
Sampson, Ian — Cleveland Way (Aurum Press Ltd 1989)
Sellers, Gladys — The Yorkshire Dales: A Walker's Guide to the National Park (Cicerone Press 1984)
Speakman, Colin — Walking in the Yorkshire Dales (Robert Hale 1982)
Spedding, Ron — Walking in Weardale (Dalesman 1977)
Spencer, Brian — Walk the North York Moors (J Bartholomew 1986)
Wainwright, Alfred — A Coast to Coast Walk (Westmorland Gazette 1973)
White, Geoffrey — Walks in Swaledale (Dalesman 1976)
White, Geoffrey — Walks in Wensleydale (Dalesman 1977)

Enjoy The Dickens Family Shopping Experience

- *Over 35,000 Home Improvement & Gardening Products*

- *Free Supervised Childrens Adventure Play Area*

- *Late Night Shopping Till 8pm Monday to Saturday*

- *Friendly & Helpful Staff*

- *Over 600 Free Car Parking Spaces*

PORTRACK LANE, STOCKTON. TEL: (0642) 679701

Index